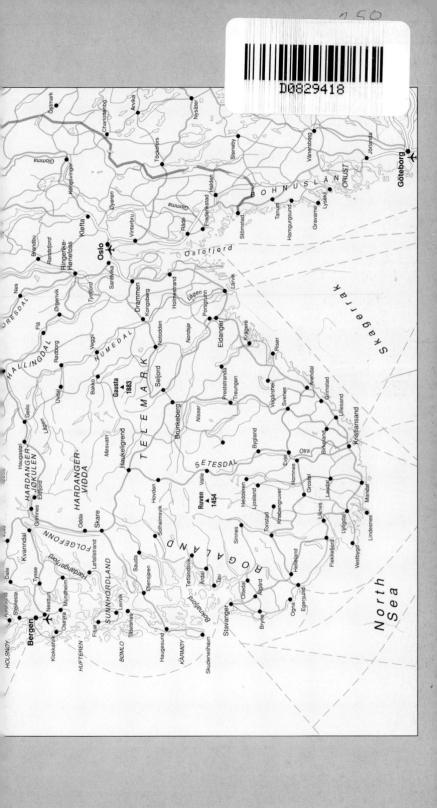

Norway, Sweden and Finland

400 km / 250 miles

Svalbard

120 km / 75 miles

INSIGHT *POCKET* GUIDES

OSLO & BERGEN

Written and Presented by **Doreen Taylor-Wilkie**

INSIGHT *POCKET* GUIDES

Insight Pocket Guide:

OSLO/BERGEN

Directed by
Hans Höfer

Managing Editor
Andrew Eames

Design Concept by
V.Barl

Design by
Gareth Walters

Printed in Singapore by
Höfer Press (Pte) Ltd
Fax: 65-8616438

Distributed in the United States by
Houghton Mifflin Company
2 Park Street
Boston, Massachusetts 02108
ISBN: 0-395-68225-8

Distributed in Canada by
Thomas Allen & Son
390 Steelcase Road East
Markham, Ontario L3R 1G2
ISBN: 0-395-68225-8

Distributed in the UK & Ireland by
GeoCenter International UK Ltd
The Viables Center, Harrow Way
Basingstoke, Hampshire RG22 4BJ
ISBN: 9-62421-544-8

Worldwide distribution enquiries:
Höfer Communications Pte Ltd
38 Joo Koon Road
Singapore 2262
ISBN: 9-62421-544-8

Velkommen!

Doreen Taylor-Wilkie

I first went to Norway in 1975, and have returned more times than I can remember. As a native of Scotland, I found a striking kinship between Norway and my own home country, even if the fjords are deeper and the mountains higher. Nestling in this superb landscape are the Norwegian cities, of which none are more intriguing than Oslo and Bergen.

Until recently Oslo was a quiet, provincial capital, where people moved soberly about their business of politics and commerce. However, the discovery of North Sea oil changed the city forever. Although its population is only half a million, Oslo buzzes with life.

Bergen's long tradition as a fishing harbour and trading station has made its citizens outgoing and cosmopolitan. During the 13th century Bergen was capital of a united Norway, and is still called the 'Fjord Capital', with its steep cobbled slopes and seven hills that hem it in to the sea.

In this book I have created a range of itineraries intended to show you the best of these cities. In both Oslo and Bergen my first three days combine to provide a full picture, and their routes are indicated on the maps provided in the relevant sections of the book. After that, I've provided diversions and excursions for visitors with a little more time and who wish to explore a little further. Don't miss the opportunity to see something of the countryside: no Norwegian city is far from endless hills, mountains, water and forest, and views that go on forever. *Velkommen – Welcome!*

Contents

Preceding pages:
Oslo on National Day

Practical Information

Following pages:
The waterfront, Bergen

HISTORY

Norway is both one of the youngest states and the oldest nations in Europe, an unknown, shadowy region until the Vikings burst out of Scandinavia just over 1,100 years ago. The sightings of their sleek ships inspired first wonder then terror along the coasts of Northern Europe. Thousands of years before, early hunters had begun to push north in the wake of the retreating icecap. As the climate warmed, they settled and became farmers, their legacy magnificent rock carvings such as those in the northernmost county of Finnmark, and a fascinating 4,000-year-old carving of a skier in Nordland, a replica of which hangs in the Ski Museum in Oslo.

Bronze Age carvings

The Vikings later became Europe's greatest explorers, adventurers and traders, venturing east as far as the Black Sea, west to Britain and France, around Scotland, to Ireland, and then north to Iceland and Greenland, reaching North America in AD1000. Later they became colonisers; anyone with a name that ends in 'son', 'sen', or 'sun' is likely to have Scandinavian ancestry.

The Vikings' skill as ship-builders was remarkable. Their longships were so fast and manoeuvrable that they could outrun any enemy, yet shallow enough to be run up on to a beach before the luckless inhabitants knew what had hit them. Three of these longships survive in the Viking Ship Museum in Oslo. Some kings and chiefs became Christian converts. Håkon den Gode was the first, a reformer and law-maker who fought hard against the heathen gods; but his imported missionaries and their sober saints had little success against the attractions of the old Norse gods. Olav Trygvasson, who followed, fared no better and it was left to King Olav Haraldson to

Culture

complete Norway's conversion. Olav lost his life at the battle of Stiklestad near Trondheim, and was recognised later as a saint, when his body was found intact with hair and nails still growing. Norway's first great cathedral, Nidaros, in Trondheim, was erected over his grave and became a place of Christian pilgrimage.

Christianity brought its industrious monk-chroniclers to keep records, but the best accounts of the Vikings come from saga writers such as the Icelander Snorre Sturluson. Undeterred by a century-long gap since the last Viking exploits, he wrote down the old tales that had passed from royal *skald* (storyteller) to *skald,* tales which laud the heroic deeds and warlike qualities of the chiefs and make splendid, if one-sided, reading.

The Vikings were a highly successful and ordered society, and, by the end of the Viking era, Norway was a great power, with colonies in Greenland, Iceland, Scotland and elsewhere. Around AD900, Harald Hårfagre successfully vanquished a mob of chieftains to become the first king of the Norwegians. Haraldshaugen, with its giant obelisk, is Norway's national monument. According to Sturlu-

The gold of the Vikings

son, the monument marks the spot where Harald Hårfagre was buried, a mile north of Haugesund on the sea route between Bergen and Stavanger.

Cultural Beginnings

Temporary peace came to Norway in the 13th century, a period of great prosperity. Under Håkon Håkonsson and his son Magnus Lagabøter (the Law-mender) the beginnings of a distinctive culture emerged in which art and religion flourished, a good example being the Baldishol Tapestry in the Museum of Applied Arts in Oslo, and the country's trade was vigorous. Then came the Black Death, which entered Norway in 1347 through Bergen, the great trading city that had brought in the wealth. At least half – some historians say two-thirds – of the population died, leaving corpses unburied and graves untended. The country starved, farms lay derelict, and fishing boats began to crumble along the shoreline.

Also instrumental in subduing Norwegian commerce was the stranglehold of the Hanseatic League, the German merchants who monopolised the trade of the north European cities in which they flourished. Though Oslo also had its Hansa merchants, Bergen was their 'capital'. The League ran Norway's trade from the Hanseatic wharfhouses in Bergen for their own profit and Norway, after a time of internal strife, sank into a union with Denmark.

Danish control followed the 'reign' of the remarkable Queen

The Baldishol Tapestry

Margrethe, a Danish princess who married King Håkon VI when she was only 10. But Norway and its monarch were impoverished and Margrethe's husband and her father, Valdemar of Denmark, often at loggerheads. When Valdemar died, Margrethe secured the future joint throne of Denmark and Norway for her son, Olav, and became monarch in all but name. The Danes invaded Sweden and, after fierce fighting and even fiercer treachery, the 1397 Kalmar Union united the three Scandinavian countries for the first and only time. The Union lasted for more than 100 years, before Sweden broke away. Norway stayed in the Union, first as a near equal partner, a status that soon deteriorated into what Norwegians call 'The Four Hundred Year Sleep,' when their country became little more than a province of Denmark.

The Big Sleep

During those somnolent centuries, Norway was converted to the Lutheran faith, grafted on by Denmark almost before Norwegians had had time to assimilate Roman Catholicism and break the last links with the fierce Norse gods. Danish links with Norway were finally severed after the Napoleonic Wars, when Frederik VI of Denmark, who had been on the losing side, was forced to hand over Norway to the Swedes as the latter's reward for supporting the allies. Norway's reaction to being handed over like a parcel from one state to another was unenthusiastic. On 17 May 1814, in a gathering at Eidsvoll, some 70km (43½ miles) north of Oslo, a hastily convened assembly hammered out a constitution which drew on the political experience of Britain, France and America. It nominated the Danish Governor of Norway, Prince Christian Frederik, as king. Oscar Wergeland's celebrated painting, *The National Assembly at Eidsvoll, 1814*, in the Storting (Parliament) in Oslo pictures the solemn scene.

In retaliation, Karl Johan of Sweden gathered 70,000 battle-hardened troops and marched into Norway. The lightly-armed Norwegians had no chance. An August armistice led to a new treaty, which put Norway under control of the Swedish crown but left the Eidsvoll Constitution intact, giving Norway its own Parliament. Nothing could stop the Norwegians turning 17 May into an annual Constitution

Line-up in front of the Storting

Day, celebrated nowadays in a whirl of Norwegian flags. In 1829, the king sent troops to break up the celebrations but, though the soldiers won that particular skirmish, the king lost the battle. By 1864, the Norwegians were singing their own national anthem, with words written by the patriot-writer Bjørnstjerne Bjørnson.

The Great Exodus

Trade suffered when the common market with Denmark disappeared but the second half of the 19th century was also a time of expansion, freer trade and the start of Norway's astonishing railway network over some of the most difficult terrain in Europe. It also saw a great exodus from Norway when thousands left the country in search of work and prosperity.

In 1825, the first emigrant boat to the New World, the 16.5m (54ft) sloop *Restauration*, left Stavanger with 52 people on board. The first 'sloopers' went largely for religious reasons but others were in search of fertile land. Many settled in Illinois and, although most outward traces of Norway have now disappeared, their influence is woven into American culture and brings Norwegian-Americans in their hundreds back to the 'old country' every summer.

Alongside emigration, re-awakened nationalism grew swiftly, fed by artists and intellectuals. Among them were the dramatist Henrik Ibsen, and writers such as Alexander Kielland and Bjørnstjerne Bjørnson. The musician Ole Bull and composer Edvard Grieg did much to revive patriotic feelings through their rediscovery of West Norway's traditional music, as did the Polar explorer Fridtjof Nansen, who became Norwegian Ambassador in London. His famous ship *Fram* forms the centrepiece of a special museum in Oslo.

Near Bergen, the homes of Grieg and Bull remain much as they left them, and Kielland's family home in Stavanger is also open to the public. Towards the end of the century, King Oskar II and the Storting disagreed. The ensuing crisis led to a referendum. The Norwegians voted overwhelmingly in favour of independence and Oskar II had little choice but abdication and retreat to Sweden.

Independence at Last

The prime minister who led Norway into independence was Christian Michelsen, a Bergen lawyer and shipowner. In 1905, Norway became an independent monarchy, with the Danish Prince Carl as elected king. Carl adopted the title King Haakon VII and for the first time in 500 years, Norway was truly its own country. The early years were exciting and prosperous, and then came World War I. Norway was determined to stay neutral and, at first, her sea trade brought great financial gains. Later, with most of her merchant fleet under charter to Britain, neutral Norway lost half its tonnage and some 2,000 merchant seamen. Their memorial stone stands alongside the fjord near the Sjøfarts (Maritime) Museum in Oslo.

Between the wars Norway was hit by the Great Depression and the Labour Party grew in popularity and strength, but its quest for equality and social welfare had to wait until after World War II. Norway's declaration of neutrality did nothing to save it. On 9 April 1940, German forces attacked and for two months the Nor-

Oslo metalworkers circa 1890

wegians fought back. There were successes such as the sinking of the German heavy cruiser *Blücher* but the odds made the outcome inevitable. The Storting refused to appoint the German's choice of governor, Vidkun Quisling, the Norwegian Nazi, whose name became a synonym for traitor. The king escaped to Britain, where the government in exile continued to function in London.

Thousands of Norwegians also escaped to fight on. There were heroic episodes, the most famous being the Norwegian commando raid on the heavy water plant at Rjukan, which ensured that Hitler lost the race for the atom bomb. The film *Heroes of Telemark* was based on this episode. Resistance brought reprisals. Akershus Fortress in Oslo became a prison and has a memorial stone to Norwegian Resistance fighters shot by the occupying Germans. It now houses the Resistance Museum. Around 40,000 were sent to prison or concentration camps such as the notorious Grini on the outskirts of Oslo.

At work on an oil platform

King Haakon returned to his country five years to the day after he left. His tireless efforts while in exile had cemented the relationship between the King and his adopted country, a bond that continued with the popular King Olav V, and his son Harald. Norwegians are extremely patriotic and on Constitution Day the capital's fervent celebrations are concentrated on the long street that leads to the Royal Palace.

After the war, Norway moved swiftly towards a political system based on the Scandinavian model of social democracy which combines capitalism with comprehensive social welfare. The country now has one of the highest standards of living in the world, with prices to match. The discovery of oil in the late 1960s took the economy almost over the top. Norway was awash with oil riches, and towns like Stavanger became international as British, French and Americans moved in. Soon the whole of the west coast, shared in the new prosperity.

Norway joined in the burst of materialism that permeated the 1980s everywhere and, today, is grappling with a period of over-dependence on oil. Fierce argument over entry to the European Community roused Norway's powerful fishing and farming interests to fury and led to a referendum in the early 1970s. The vote went against membership but it may be that the 1990s will see the Norwegians inside the Community. If so, it will only be after a struggle, as hard fought as those of the 19th-century.

Historical Outline

Prehistory Norway settled by primitive hunting communities, about whom little is known.

AD

793 Vikings attack Lindisfarne, off the east coast of England. Viking raiders reached most of Europe in the next 200 years.

9th century Harald Hårfagre creates political organisation and becomes first king of Norway. Christianity gradually accepted.

1028–35 Period of Danish rule, followed by civil war.

1066 Harald Hårdråda mounts an expedition to claim the English throne, but is himself killed in battle.

13th century A period of peace and prosperity under Håkon Håkonsson and his son Magnus Lagabøter (the Law-mender). Trade flourishes through membership of the Hanseatic league.

1262 Iceland and Greenland accept Norwegian sovereignty.

1347 The Black Death sweeps through Norway, killing up to two-thirds of the population.

1397 The Union of Kalmar brings Norway, Sweden and Denmark together under a single monarch. Danish Lutheranism becomes prevalent in Norway.

1523 The Union is dissolved, but Norway continues to be ruled by Danish governors. Norway enters what it calls the Four Hundred Year Sleep, during which time timber and fish become the mainstays of the economy.

1814 A Norwegian assembly at Eidsvoll creates a national constitution and the Storting (parliament). Constitution Day (17 May) becomes the most important day in the Norwegian calendar. In retaliation, Karl Johan of Sweden invades Norway, encountering little resistance. Norway is ceded to Sweden, but its own parliament is allowed to remain intact.

1825 The first ship leaves for the New World, starting a massive emigration. Nationalism begins to take root.

1828 The playwright Henrik Ibsen is born.

1884 The Storting is given real power.

1898 Universal male suffrage is granted.

1905 Union with Sweden is finally dissolved. Danish Prince Carl becomes King Haakon VII. A liberal government introduces women's suffrage and social reform, as well as maintaining neutrality during World War I.

1920 Norway becomes a member of the League of Nations.

1940 Germany invades Norway in the early years of World War II. The King escapes to Britain. Puppet government imposed under Vidkun Quisling, whose name becomes a synonym for traitor.

1945 The monarch and government-in-exile return after the end of the war. Norway is one of the founding signatories of the United Nations (UN), and goes on to join the North Atlantic Treaty Organisation (NATO).

1960s The discovery of oil in the North Sea helps to boost the Norwegian economy.

1972 Led by fishing and farming interests, Norway decides against joining the European Community (EC) following a referendum.

1980s Oil wealth brings undreamed of prosperity.

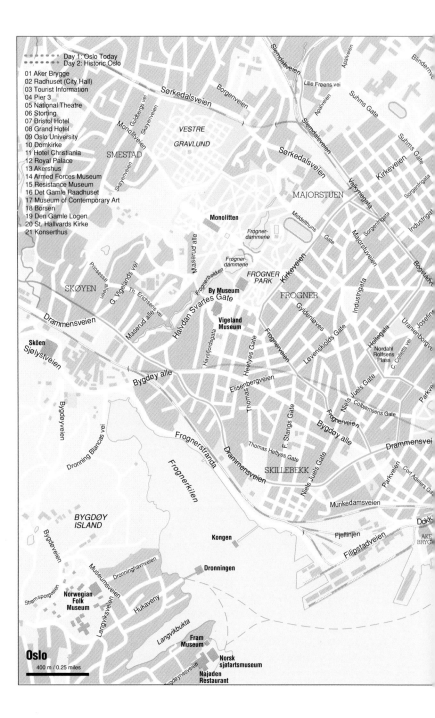

Day 1: Oslo Today
Day 2: Historic Oslo

01 Aker Brygge
02 Radhuset (City Hall)
03 Tourist Information
04 Pier 3
05 National Theatre
06 Storting
07 Bristol Hotel
08 Grand Hotel
09 Oslo University
10 Domkirke
11 Hotel Christiania
12 Royal Palace
13 Akershus
14 Armed Forces Museum
15 Resistance Museum
16 Det Gamle Raadhuset
17 Museum of Contemporary Art
18 Borsen
19 Den Gamle Logen
20 St. Hallvards Kirke
21 Konserthus

VESTRE
GRAVLUND

SMESTAD

MAJORSTUEN

Monolitten

Frogner-
dammene

Frogner-
dammene

FROGNER
PARK

FROGNER

SKØYEN

By Museum
Gate

Vigeland
Museum

Drammensveien

Sköen
Sjølystveien

Bygdøy alle

Elisenbergveien

Frognerstranda

Drammensveien

SKILLEBEKK

Drammensvei

BYGDØY
ISLAND

Munkedamsveien

Kongen

Fjellinjen

Filipstadveien

Dokk

AKE
BRYG

Dronningen

Norwegian
Folk
Museum

Langvikbukta

Fram
Museum

Norsk
sjøfartsmuseum

Najaden
Restaurant

Oslo
400 m / 0.25 miles

Oslo is one of the most manageable capitals in the world, with a compact centre easy to wander through and masses of green open spaces. The Danish King Christian IV can take the credit for laying the modern city's foundations in 1624 but 7,000 years earlier its enviable position at the head of the Oslofjord had attracted first hunters then farmers and traders.

Oslo wharf

Early Oslo, built by Harald Hårdråda in the 11th century, lay to the east of the modern city. Håkon V Magnusson, who made Oslo his capital 200 years later, built a fortress on the site of the Akershus Slot. In 1624, the wood-built town burned to the ground and was rebuilt by Christian IV under the walls of Akershus Slot. Called Christiania after its founder, its lattice of wide streets forms the basis of modern Oslo. Freedom from Denmark brought a flourish of fine 19th-century buildings. The city spread westwards towards the parliament building, the Storting, the new Royal Palace and beyond. During the last decade Oslo has changed its style from small, sleepy capital to bustling city.

Oslo is a 'green' city, which means you pay to bring in a car. The centre is easy to get around on foot and the integrated transport systems – bus, local train, tram, ferry – whisk you in less than half an hour into the hills, forests and fjords. For serious sight-seeing invest in an *Oslokartet* (Oslo Card), valid for one, two or three days, at a cost of around 100–180NKR. For transport queries, try the *Rutebok for Oslo* available from Trafikanten, at Jernbanetorget (see *Practical Information*).

1. Oslo Today

A morning walk from the central thoroughfare Karl Johans Gate to the Stortorvet marketplace, the Domkirke (Cathedral) and its park. From the National Theatre and the Storting (parliament) to lunch at Aker Brygge or a Karl Johans Gate café. For the afternoon, a Fjord Cruise. Dinner in the Atrium, Royal Christiania Hotel. Smuget or Stortorvets Gjæstgiveri for late-night music.

Few Oslonians would deny that the best approach to Oslo is by boat, up the fjord to the busy harbour. Failing that, make an early sight-seeing tour by water. Most tour boats and some ferries leave from **Pipervika**, the harbour in the heart of the city. Opposite Pipervika is **Rådhuset**, the City Hall, a massive russet-coloured building with two huge square towers, typical of the 1930s.

To reach Rådhuset from **Karl Johans Gate** (the central thoroughfare) turn south into **Rosenkrantz Gate** and head for the sea to reach **Rådhusgata**, then turn right. This is much less complicated than it sounds because, from most places in central Oslo, the

Colour in Oslo's city centre

City Hall is hard to miss. The **Tourist Information Office** (Tel: 83-00-50) is in the yellow building to the right (Vestbane Station).

Walk back up to Karl Johans Gate once more, and stroll along this broad pedestrian street. Karl Johans Gate is the main artery of modern Oslo and leads from Jernbanetorget with Oslo S (Oslo Sentral) at the eastern end, right up to the Royal Palace at the other. For much of its length, it is free of vehicles and crowds browse along pavements crowded with gaudy little stalls.

The area has some of Oslo's best restaurants, and cafés that move outside in summer. There are also time-honoured hotels such as the Grand with an excellent view of the comings and goings of the Storting (parliament) when it is in session, the Hotel Bristol just around the corner in Christian IV's Gate and the Hotel Continental across the **Studenterlunden** park on **Stortings Gata**, which runs

View from the Karl Johans Gate

parallel to Karl Johans Gate. This 19th-century heart of modern Oslo is built on an easy-to-follow grid system with parks and gardens lying between the two main streets.

From the pedestrian end nearest to Jernbanetorget, you come almost immediately to **Stortorvet**, the market place, with its bright stalls of flowers. On one side is the **Domkirke** (the cathedral) consecrated in 1697, after a fire destroyed its predecessor. The ruins of an even earlier cathedral, **St Hallvard's**, named after Oslo's patron saint, lie to the east of the city at **Gamle Oslo**, where the first city stood. Before going in, take a look at the stone relief to the right of the main entrance. It is believed to have come from St Hallvard's, and dates from around AD1100. The 1718 tower clock is Norway's oldest. The bronze doors of the main entrance, which illustrate the Beatitudes, are by Dagfinn Werenskiold, and were added in 1938.

Inside, the cathedral is all greys, blues, greens and gilt against dazzling white, and very Scandinavian. Though the interior owes its appearance mainly to a restoration completed in 1950, this clear brilliance is typified by the organ front which now surrounds a modern organ. The stained glass windows are the work of Emanuel Vigeland. But it is the ceilings that compel the eye. Painted 1936–50 by Hugo Louis Mohr, they show Biblical scenes such as the Flood and the Destruction of Sodom and Gomorrah, and episodes in the life of Christ.

The National Theatre

Behind the Cathedral is **Domkirkeparken** (6.30am–9pm), a peaceful, sheltered spot where you can sit outside at **Café Cappuccino**. The garden is screened by the red-brick arcade of **Basarhallene**, a semi-circular wall of little shops, galleries, and cafés. Some of the cafés, such as the late-night **Café Bacchus**, are open until at least 1am (except on Sunday).

Back along Karl Johans Gate, the **Storting**, built in the 1860s, looks over the small park of **Løvebakken** (the Lion's Hill) to the **National Theatre** and, with perhaps unconscious symbolism, towards the Royal Palace. When the Storting is sitting, the public galleries are open to the public. Between mid to late June and the end of September, when the government is in recess, there are daily tours at 11am, noon, and 1pm, led by a guide who explains the parliamentary system simply and shows you the two main debating chambers, the **Odelsting** and the **Lagting**.

Between the Storting and the National Theatre is Studenterlunden, the Students' Park, situated opposite the main university building. In July only, the Great Hall of the University (where the Nobel Peace Prize is awarded) with its celebrated murals by Edvard Munch, is open between noon and 2pm.

The National Theatre is a beautiful building, the heart of Oslo's theatre life. In the surrounding garden are statues of the writers Henrik Ibsen and Bjørnstjere Bjørnson. To Oslonians, the National Theatre is Ibsen's theatre. (Ask at the Tourist Information Centre about plans for a special Ibsen tour to include the theatre and his Oslo flat near the Royal Palace.) Unfortunately for visitors, almost

Oslo University

Steel and glass at Aker Brygge

all National Theatre plays are presented in Norwegian, except during the September **Ibsen Festival** when foreign companies perform in their own languages. At other times it could still be worth visiting, if only for the sheer magnificence of the auditorium. The theatre houses a rare collection of portraits of famous artistes and dramatists by well known Norwegian painters such as Munch, Krohg, Werenskiold, and Sørensen. There is an English-language guided tour on Fridays at 5.30pm, from mid-August to mid-June.

Ahead is the Royal Palace, with parks on either side open to the public. The palace itself, with a dominating statue of King Karl Johan in front, is not open but there is daily a **Changing the Guard**

A rest and a chat

at 1.30pm. When the King is in residence, the Royal Guards' band plays on weekdays.

There are two choices for a quick lunch before the **Fjord Cruise**. Either try one of the cafés and restaurants along Karl Johans Gate, such as **Henrikke** on Studenterlunden, or turn down one of the streets leading to the water, Roald Amundsen's Gate or Rosenkrantz Gate, to the glass and steel of **Aker Brygge**, facing the sea on the right of the City Hall. Aker Brygge was built on to the wharfhouses that once lined the quay, two of them still stand, though the old seamen, clambering ashore, would never have recognised these light and airy buildings, where the temperature hardly changes from summer to winter.

24

Aker Brygge is Oslo's newest temple to leisure and has two theatres – one modern, one experimental – and several other arts projects and schools. But its aim is to become a living community and it contains flats and houses. On a sunny summer day, it makes a fine place for lunch beside the water. The heart is **Festplassen** which faces the sun and the marina. If it is too cold outside, you can see it all through wide glass windows. The choice of lunch is boundless, ranging from a sandwich and a beer or coffee to a full meal.

Make sure to finish lunch in time to reach **Pier 3** on the quay in front of the City Hall, from where the boat leaves at 3.30pm (book through Båtservice Sightseeing, Tel: 20-07-15). This two-hour Fjord Cruise sweeps out through the harbour, where large ferries, cruise boats, and cargo ships attest to Norway's long standing preoccupation with the sea, and the forests of masts show just how much Norwegians love the water.

As the boat heads out, on the peninsula to the left is Akershus, a medieval fortress still in use by the military. Look behind to the hill and forest rising behind central Oslo and the graceful white scoop of the **Holmenkollen Ski Jump**, heart of the annual Holmenkollen Ski Festival. For the next couple of hours, the boat weaves through islands and narrow sounds which form the background to Oslo's summer life. This cruise service runs from May through late September. A **50-minute mini-cruise** also leaves on the hour from 10am–8pm and there are various lunch and evening buffet cruises, when you may go ashore to eat, or tackle prawns on board. Times vary with the seasons, so enquire before you decide.

Have dinner at the **Atrium Café** in the **Royal Christiania Hotel** (Tel: 42-94-10), in **Biskop Gunnerusgate**, just opposite Oslo Sentral. The Atrium in this recently modernised hotel is a central glass-covered arcade, complete with trees and plants. Take one of

The Henrikke café in central Oslo

The Storting

the glass-sided 'crawler' lifts which ride up and down the side of
the Atrium to obtain the best view.

In Norwegian terms, this is a medium priced restaurant and you
need spend no more than around 150NKR per person without wine.
The hotel has at least three more eating places, including the elegant (and pricey) **Christian den 4**, the **Bacchus Vinbar**, and a
disco in the **Offside Pub**, which you could try later.

After eating, wander off in search of some music to **Smuget** (Tel:
42-52-02), whose nightly programme ranges from jazz to blues and
rock, fortunately on different floors, and stays open until 4am. To
find it at Kirkegate 34, turn left off Karl Johans Gate, near the
Domkirke, and go through the courtyard. An alternative is **Stortorvet Gæstgiveri** (Tel: 42-88-63), an authentic old inn with several rooms, which some nights becomes a jazz pub.

2. Historic Oslo

A walk through Christiania (old Oslo) past Borsen and Gamle Logen towards Akersnes (promontory) above the harbour. To the Akershus Castle and Fortress and the Resistance Museum. Lunch at the Engebret Café, followed by an afternoon in the Museum of Contemporary Art. In the evening, a concert at Konserthus, followed by dinner in Det Gamle Raadhuset.

Christiania, named after that great builder-king Christian IV of Denmark and Norway, came into being in 1624, when the medieval city of Oslo, across the bay below Ekeberg Hill, burnt down. Christian designed what he hoped would be a fire-proof city with roads 15m (49ft) wide, laid in a grid pattern with buildings of stone or half-timber only. It says a lot for Christian's skill as a planner that the road system still forms the heart of central Oslo, though few of the original buildings remain.

From a starting point at Jernbanetorget, turn left into Fred Olsens Gate and walk along past **Borsen**, the old Stock Exchange. Still in use today, it was designed in the 1820s by the architect Christian H Grosch, who was also responsible for planning much of the expanded city. Not far away in Myntgate, **Den Gamle Logen**, which has been used for festive occasions for the last 150 years, is once again a concert hall.

The city's careful design is made even clearer when you see the **Christiania Bymodell**, situated under the walls of Akershus Slot. To reach it, turn right into **Rådhusgate** past No 19, a restaurant and art gallery to which we will be returning later, left into Kongensgate past Bankplassen, where you will be lunching, and right into Myntgate. Continue until you come to the long, low building

The Stock Exchange

Sunbathing war veteran

known as **Høymagasinet** (Hay Barn), which houses the Bymodell. This model of Christiania as it looked in 1838 spreads over an area of 10 x 15m (33 x 49ft), which gives a three-dimensional view of the city. Look closely and, opposite Raadmannsgården, you will find **Det Gamle Raadhuset** (the Old City Hall; Tel: 42-01-07) at Nedre Slotsgate 1, another of the oldest buildings, where you will eat tonight. There is also a 20-minute screen presentation which traces Christiania's development from 1624–1840.

Just a few steps on from Høymagasinet, turn into **Kirkegate** and the main entrance to Akershus Slot. At the lower end beside the parade ground and the Armed Forces Museum is a monument to the victims of World War II. A gigantic woman and a small man in the circle of the earth symbolise his death and her continuing life and struggle. The sculptor was Gunnar Jansson. The **Armed Forces Museum** (Tel: 40-35-82/40-37-69) nearby houses the Buick in which Crown Prince Olav (later King Olav) toured Oslo on his triumphant return after World War II, and some of the tiny aircraft that struggled so bravely against insuperable odds. It also has the only cafeteria in the area, a good place for a quick stop.

The Akershus stronghold

The Resistance Museum

The first castle at **Akershus**, with a big central tower, was built around AD1300 by Håkon V Magnusson, and commands the whole of the bay and fjord. In the early 17th century, Christian IV rebuilt the fortress as a royal castle and, thanks to restoration early this century, much of the fortification looks today as it must have done back then. Inside there is a long courtyard with a tower at each end, and **Olav's Hall** (Tel: 41-25-21), used as a prison in World War II for members of the Norwegian Resistance. The castle is also a royal mausoleum, with the tombs of King Haakon VII, Queen Maud and Crown Princess Martha, alongside those of Sigurd Jorsalfarer and Håkon V Magnusson, the builder.

The **Resistance Museum** (Tel: 40-31-38) is in a part of the castle known as the **Double Battery** and the **Frame House**. It is effectively laid out, starting with cuttings from the September 1938 meeting between Neville Chamberlain, the British Prime Minister, and Hitler in Munich and ends with pictures of the joyous liberation. Between are records of heroism and touchingly simple personal accounts. The museum stands next to the memorial to the 42 Resistance members who were executed there. At the end of World War II, for a short period Norway restored the death penalty. The traitor Vidkun Quisling was sentenced to death and shot at Akershus.

Lunch at **Engebret Café** (Tel: 33-66-94) on Bankplassen, a restaurant as old as the district itself, can be inside or outdoor, large or small – a *smørbrød* between 11am and 3pm (from 3pm–10.30pm the restaurant is à la carte) – but it is all good. My apple cake came not only with cream but with a rose!

Across the square is the **Museum of Contemporary Art** (Tel: 33-58-20), opened in 1990 in what was formerly the Bank of Norway's headquarters; a gracious building of Norwegian granite and marble, it was designed in 1906 by the architect I O Hjort, who was much influenced by the wave of nationalism following Norway's secession from the union with Sweden.

The museum now holds all the postwar collections transferred from the National Gallery and Norway's State Travelling Gallery. Probably the best known

Colourful traditional costumes

internationally of the contemporary painters exhibited are Jacob Weideman – his work is also in the Musée National d'Art Moderne in Paris – and Anna-Eva Bornman, whose work hangs in many European collections. Of them all, Arne Ekeland is widely considered to be the most important. The museum's principal sculptors are Arnold Haukeland, Knut Steen, and Nils Aas. (You can also see sculptures by both Haukeland and Aas in Bergen on Ventre Stromkai and in the Teaterparken.)

My suggestion for your evening is to go to Oslo's **Konserthus**, (Concert Hall; Tel: 83-32-00; box office Tel: 83-54-10). The Konserthus is the home of the Oslo Philharmonic, conducted by Mariss Janson, in residence from early September to June each year. Here you can also hear popular artistes such as Joan Armatrading or one of the rock greats. **Den Gamle Logen** (Tel: 33-22-60), **Akershus Castle** (Tel: 41-25-21) and the **University Aula** (Great Hall; Tel: 42-90-91 ext 756), among others, also have classical music performances in the summer, which usually start around 7.30pm. Summer is also Oslo's time for festivals of all sorts, from opera and chamber music to theatre and jazz. Even if you are not a folklore addict, sample the music and costumes of Norwegian folklore in the small auditorium of the Konserthus on Mondays and Thursdays during July and most of August.

For dinner, **Det Gamle Raadhuset** (the Old City Hall) is one of the oldest houses in Christiania which, in the past, has done duty as courtroom and dungeon, assembly rooms, concert hall and even as a place for church services. In 1856 it was sold to Matheus Helseth who opened it as a restaurant. Today, the present owners have done much to restore the building, with a restaurant in the former wine cellars. It is particularly well known for fish and shellfish, and a two-course meal will cost between 200–250NKR per person, without wine.

3. Bygdøy Day

Ferry or bus to the island of Bygdøy to see the Norwegian Folk Museum and Viking Ship Museum. Lunch at the Najaden Restaurant in the Sjøfartsmuseum (Maritime Museum). On to the Kon Tiki and Ra Museum. Finally to the Fram Museum before the boat or bus back. Dinner at a choice of grand hotel restaurants, followed by a visit to a nightclub.

The Bygdøy ferry leaves from Pier 3 in front of the City Hall (same pier as Itinerary 1) and you get off at **Dronningen**, the boat's first stop on Bygdøy. (By bus, take the No 30, marked Bygdøy, from the National Theatre and ask for the Folk Museum.) Once off the boat, take note of **Lanternen Kro** (Tel: 43-81-25) a traditional old inn, as a possible lunch alternative to **Najaden** (Tel: 43-81-80), though it will mean returning to this point after the museum tours.

Walk up the hill (**Huk Aveny**) to a turning on the right, well signed for the **Norwegian Folk Museum** (Tel: 43-70-20). Scandinavians love their outdoor folk museums, large collections of buildings showing a way of life that lasted longer here than in many other parts of Europe. This one was founded in 1894 when, in areas such as Setesdal, the way of life depicted was only just begin-

Traditional house in the Folk Museum

The Norwegian Folk Museum

ning to change. This brings a rare authenticity to the 170 old buildings from more than 20 different areas of Norway.

Norway's vast distances meant that farms were scattered, and there were few villages with a large number of houses. A group of buildings in the museum will usually turn out to be the component parts – store, kitchen, *stua* (living room), loft – of one farm. These beautiful, dark wooden buildings with their carved exterior galleries and stairs, are not only from rural areas. There is a waiting room for steamship passengers from Pipervika in Oslo, old mills, and a stave church from 1200.

Return to the main road, turn right and the **Viking Ship Museum** (Tel: 43-83-79) is only a short and pleasant walk. The three longships found in the Oslofjord area all ended their careers as burial ships and contained a wealth of the household implements, jewellery and weaponry that the Vikings considered necessary in the afterlife. They are the Tune ship, found 1867, the Gokstad ship, excavated 1880, and the Oseberg ship, discovered in 1904; probably the oldest of the three; it was built around AD800.

The Gokstad ship was the best preserved, complete with the skeleton of its royal chief. The ship was built of oak, is 24m (80ft) long, and was originally designed for sailing and fighting. The Oseberg ship, slightly smaller but with a burial chamber luxurious

Folk-dancing in traditional costume

enough to indicate royalty, held skeletons of two women. This may have been the grave of Queen Åsa, the only known queen in the early Yngling dynasty, and her bondswoman. A modern replica of the Gokstad ship recently made a successful crossing to New York. According to the ancient Sagas, whose statements are now backed by modern archaeology, the Vikings made the same voyage almost 1,000 years before when Leif Eriksson discovered Vinland den Gode (the land of good pasture) his name for North America, in a foray from Greenland in AD1000.

The walk down to **Bygdøynes** is quite a hike but has the bonus that you can call in and look at the old **Sjømanskirke**, facing the sea. This is rarely open but if you ring the bell the custodian will almost certainly let you have a look. The alternative, once again, is bus No 30 from the Viking ships to Bygdøynes.

At Bygdøynes, the ferry terminal, the first things you notice are the fore-and-aft schooner *Svanen*, not just part of the museum but a floating centre for youth clubs and school children; and the polar vessel *Gjøa*, once a seal-hunter. *Gjøa* was Roald Amundsen's vessel for his epic journey through the Northwest Passage. He left in 1903 and it was August 1906 before *Gjøa* forced a way through, excellent preparation for Amundsen's meticulously planned and successful attempt on the South Pole when, by just a month, he beat the British team led by Captain Scott. Before tackling the museums proper, there is time for lunch at **Najaden**, part of the **Sjøfartsmuseum** (Maritime Museum; Tel: 43-82-40), where you will find Norwegian specialities and a good cold table.

The sea and the long coast have been a constant link in Norway's social history and the Maritime Museum aims to show much of it, from the model of the Kvaldor boat, a dugout from AD600, to a vessel of the mid-19th century (*Kong Sverre* built at Horten), and finally to a modern tanker. *Kong Sverre* displaced 3,500 tons and was the largest and most powerfully armed wooden warship built in Scandinavia. The Boat Hall, in a separate building opposite the main entrance houses many of the small boats that were as characteristic of their districts as the distinctive regional wooden houses and national costumes in the Folk Museum. Closer to the ferry is the joint **Kon-Tiki and Ra Museum** (Tel: 48-80-50), and Fridtjof Nansen's

The Viking Ship Museum

The Fram caught in pack ice

Fram. I always leave the **Fram Museum** (Tel: 43-83-70) to last because, of all maritime museums, it is the most atmospheric.

In 1947, Thor Heyerdahl's feat in building a balsa raft, the *Kon-Tiki*, and sailing it across the Pacific grabbed the imagination of a world tired of war. It brought him world fame and still draws many to see the raft, well displayed on two floors. Part of the same building holds *Ra II*, Heyerdahl's second craft, a reed boat built in Egypt at the foot of the Giza pyramids, and used to test a theory that this sort of boat could have reached the West Indies long before Columbus.

The *Fram* made three remarkable voyages through the ice and yet there she stands, sturdy and trim and freshly painted, in the museum specially built for her in 1935. Round the walls of the hall are artefacts and documents from the ship's remarkable history. Her first voyage was disastrous: three years spent stuck in pack ice. Otto Sverdrup led *Fram's* second expedition to the islands north of Arctic Canada, and in 1910, Amundsen took the ship south for his onslaught on the South Pole.

As you climb the gangway it hardly seems possible that this spick and span ship could ever have been covered in cobwebs of frost and endured the pressure of the 'ice-quakes'. Today, she is scrubbed and polished with cabins and their contents still intact. Before you leave

Ra II goes to sea

A statue guards the Theatercaféen

Bygdøynes, walk down to the point to see **Joseph Grimeland's memorial** to the 4,500 Norwegian sailors who perished during World War II. Near it is the **Mine Box**, a monument to the 2,100 Norwegian merchant seamen who lost their lives in World War I.

Dinner at **Theatercaféen** or the **Grand Café** has atmosphere whichever one you chose. Theatercaféen, (Tel: 33-32-00), in the Hotel Continental across Stortings Gata from the National Theatre, is in 1900s style, with heavy draped curtains, marble-topped tables with plush bench seats and a glassed-in verandah over the street, open from spring to autumn. On a Friday or Saturday night it would be wise to book. Theatercaféen is famous as a haunt of actors, artists and the intelligentsia and the walls are studded with portraits and pencil sketches of many of Norway's leading artistes of the past and present. The food is straightforward and as good as befits a hotel whose upstairs restaurant, **Annen Étage** (Tel: 41-90-60), is one of the most famous in Norway.

The Grand Café (Tel: 42-93-90) in the Grand Hotel on Karl Johans Gate was a haunt of Oslo's 19th-century Bohemians. On the far wall is a huge mural painted by **Per Krohg**, showing a gathering of admirers as Ibsen arrives for lunch. The menu will certainly include some Norwegian specialities and this could be the place to try reindeer, which is a bit like venison and very tender.

Nightclubs open and close with monotonous frequency in Oslo and it is always risky to recommend other than the most established. If you like jazz, you will not go wrong with **Rockefeller** (Tel: 20-32-32; open until 4am on Thursday, Friday and Saturday, a little earlier the rest of the week, closed on Sunday) in Torgata 16 (enter from Marieboesgt) with which Miles Davies was much involved. Its annual high spot is the Jazz Festival in August.

4. In the Marka

A day in the open air of the Nordmarka – forest, hill and lake – to see Tryvannstårnet, Holmenkollen and the ski jump.

The whole of central Oslo is surrounded by an area of forest, lakes, hills and moor known as the Marka. It is ideal for winter skiing, summer walking, canoeing and fishing – particularly the accessible Nordmarka, which is dotted with *markastuer*, places where you can eat, rest and, in some cases, find accommodation.

Cross-country skiing is a national winter sport and on Sundays whole families are out in the Marka with tiny babies securely

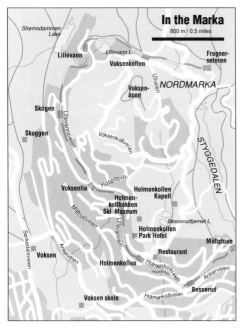

wrapped behind the windshields of their *pulker* (little sledges). In summer, you can combine walking with stops at Tryvannstårnet and the Holmenkollen ski jump. Take T-bane train No 15 from **Stortinget** underground station to **Frognerseteren**, from where a network of clearly marked paths leads out into the Nordmarka. The one for **Tryvannstårnet** takes around 15–20 minutes. The drive from central Oslo to the top takes around the same time but the walk is part of the day's outing.

Tryvannstårnet is not only Oslo's radio and telephone tower, but it also affords the best view in Southern Norway. Get into a lift which rises nearly 118m (387ft) in a surging 11 seconds. From the observation platform, you are nearly 588m (1,929ft) above sea level and the view is magnificent. On a good day, it covers around 30,000km^2 (18,000 square miles) and over to the east you can see as far as Sweden. South is Oslo and the fjord islands and in every other direction stretches of open land and forests seem to go on forever. Below, the tower has a shop and refreshments.

The easiest way to go down to **Holmenkollen** is to follow the road to **Voksenkollen** station to the corner where it meets Holmenkollveien. Looking towards the great ski jump you will see the pool area which is used in summer for concerts. The alternative way down is longer. Follow the track signed Frognerseteren past **Øvresetertjern** lake and down through the forest to the 100-year-old **Frognerseteren Restaurant** (Tel: 14-08-90/14-37-36), which

Tryvannstårnet

offers an excellent *koldtbord*, the traditional lavish cold table. There are wooden tables outside where people eat their own picnics. From here, take the marked forest route to the left of the main road down to Holmenkollen until the track crosses the road just above **Holmenkollen Kapell**.

The **Holmenkollen Ski Jumping Competition**, which is held in March each year, started in 1892 and is the oldest in the world. The last day has the Great Ski Jump when the crowd is so huge that it seems Oslo must be empty. To get a feel for the jump (but only if you like heights) go first to the top of the jumping tower. Tickets are on sale next door in the **Ski Museum** (Tel: 14-16-90). There is a lift but the last stairway before the top is a steep climb.

The Ski Museum's earliest known relic is a copy of the 4,000-year-old rock carving of a skier from Rødøy in Nordland, and the exhibition ranges over the development of skiing in every part of Norway. There are tableaux of Amundsen's and Nansen's expeditions and a history of royal skiing, as well as a tribute to **Sondre Norheim**, the father of modern skiing.

Holmenkollen Restaurant (Tel: 14-62-26), near the Museum, has wonderful views and serves good Norwegian dishes. The nearby Holmenkollen Cafeteria sells *smørbrød* (open sandwiches). The walk down to the Holmenkollen station takes 10 minutes, and within half an hour you are back in the city.

Norwegians are passionate skiers

5. Vigeland and the By Museum

A morning's visit, to the Vigeland park at Frogner (not to be confused with Frognerseteren), the Vigeland Museum and the nearby Oslo By Museum (City Museum).

Go first to **Frogner** which holds the bulk of Gustav **Vigeland's** masterpieces, five great groups of figures, linked together along an axis over 850m (930yds) long. Vigeland was born into a wood-carving family in **Mandal** on the south coast and as a young man went to Oslo to learn wood carving and sculpture. He held his first independent exhibition in 1894 when he was only 25. Vigeland was a good negotiator. In 1921, he struck a deal with the City of Oslo by which he donated all his works of art in return for a studio, which is now the **Vigeland Museum** (Tel: 44-23-06).

Take a No 9 tram or buses 72 or 73 and ask for the Vigeland Park main entrance. Through these big gates, the path runs up to a bridge, lined with 58 bronze statues of human figures. From the left-hand side of the bridge can be seen a carved circle of children in relaxed poses. The bridge leads to the great bowl of the fountain, held up by six male figures and surrounded by a mosaic of black and white granite. Beyond and above is **Monoliten** (the Monolith) Vigeland's most famous work. Carved in granite from a single stone it depicts human figures, groping towards the sky. The Monolith is the centrepiece of a hill, encircled by tiers of steps with 12 groups of figures on them, showing the cycle of life from childhood to death. The park's final sculpture is the Wheel of Life, a group of seven colossal figures.

On the way to the Vigeland Museum, just outside the park and across **Halvdan Svartes Gate**, call in at the **By Museum** (Tel: 43-06-45), Oslo's city museum which lies in the lovely old Frogner Manor. The main building, which dates from 1790, shows city interiors and paintings; other exhibits round the courtyard are based on themes such as town planning and trade, illustrating how recently Norway became a modern industrialised country.

The museum has a photograph of the finest building in the so-called 'English quarter', just past the **Royal Park** on Drammen-

The monolith in Vigeland park

High flying in the park

veien, where Oslo's first examples of late French Renaissance style rose in the 1880s. Sadly, this building has been replaced by a hideous 1960s block; in front of it is a statue of Winston Churchill.

On the way back to the town centre, look for the statue on your right just after the two main roads join. A little further into the centre is the Nobel Building, where the winner of the Peace Prize is decided. Though Nobel was a Swede, the countries were still united at the turn of the century when he inaugurated the scheme and decreed that Norway should award the Prize.

Finally, call in at the **Vigeland Museum**. It has over 1,500 sculptures, 430 woodcuts, more than 400 plates, 12,000 drawings, and in the region of 11,000 sketches. On summer evenings, there are sometimes concerts in the museum courtyard.

6. The Munch Museum and Botanic Garden

An afternoon's visit to see the enormous collection of the works of Norway's greatest painter, and the Botanic Garden.

To reach the **Munch Museum** (Tel: 67-37-74) at Tøyen, take bus No 29 from Jernbanetorget or the T-bane (underground) train No 5 from Stortinget to Tøyen. The museum lies opposite Tøyenhagen, which houses the **Oslo Botanic Garden**.

Munch and Vigeland were almost the same age. They became friends in Berlin and remained so until they both fell in love with the same woman, Dagny Juel, also a painter. Munch despised Vigeland's bargain with the City of Oslo (see Itinerary 5) and donated all his own work to Oslo on his death in 1944. It includes 1,100 paintings and 18,000 prints as well as 4,500 drawings, plates, and many letters, so much material that the exhibition is constantly changing. Munch returned to the same themes in different forms, so that a painting you come across in the National Gallery may be similar but not identical to one on display in the Munch Museum.

Munch self-portrait

39

Munch and Vigeland came from very different backgrounds. Munch's was comfortable and intellectual; his father was a doctor, and an uncle who was one of the leading historians of his age. But his mother died early, and something of his father's gloomy nature communicated itself to the boy. One of Munch's most famous subjects, *The Sick Child*, was inspired by his sister's death. Munch started as a Naturalist and, after a short period as an Impressionist, he became recognised as a strong pioneering influence on Expressionism throughout Europe. After a mental breakdown early in the century, he moved to landscape painting then, as he recovered, he gradually returned to Expressionism. This period, around 1916, saw the completion of his great murals for the University Aula, and his sketches for *The Sun* and *Alma Mater* also date from the years after his illness.

Best known of his earlier works is his *Life Cycle: Puberty*, *The Kiss*, *Anxiety*, *Melancholy*, *Death in the Sickroom* and *The Sick Child*. Some are in the museum, others were sold during his lifetime. Very striking is the *Death of Marat*, to which Munch brought his own experience of betrayal.

The Museum restaurant serves traditional Norwegian dishes which you could sample before a visit to the oasis of the **Botanic Gardens**, which close at 8pm in summer, and **Museum**. The gardens have beautiful, exotic species and more than 1,000 mountain plants. If the appetite for works of art is not yet sated, view **Dagny Tande Lid's** art exhibition inside the museum.

If you wanted to devote a day to this Munch/Botanic Gardens visit, you could reverse the order and visit Tøyenhagen in the morning and include the **Zoological**, and **Mineral and Geological museums**, both in the same gardens but closed by mid-afternoon. Unlike most museums, the Munch stays open until 6pm in summer.

Rest after exhausting sight-seeing

7. Art and Museums

The National Gallery, Rådhuset or the City Hall, the Historical Museum and the Museum of Applied Art.

This has to be a morning trip because the galleries and museums close at 3–4pm, and the City Hall at 2pm. The locations are within easy walking distance from Karl Johans Gate.

Start with the **National Gallery** (opens at 10am), which holds the state's largest collection of paintings, sculptures and graphic art. This is the place to trace the great surge of 19th-century Norwegian painting, prompted mainly by feelings of nationalism. The Norwegian contribution to the National Romantic movement was typified by painters such as Adolph Tidemand and Hans Gude. Their most famous picture *Brudeferd i Hardanger* (Bridal Journey in Hardanger) may now seem over-theatrical, but its four versions were enormously popular at the time. There is also a whole room devoted to Edvard Munch, which includes his most famous picture, *The Scream.* In order not to miss the 11am guided tour of the City Hall, concentrate on the Norwegian work, though the gallery has a wonderful collection of European painters including Rubens, El Greco, Cézanne, Degas, Braque and Picasso. If you opt for all these riches, the next City Hall tour is at noon, the last one at 1pm.

Rådhuset (City Hall) was Oslo's main contribution to the flood of projects which followed Norway's new nationhood. Planned in 1915 and begun in 1931, it is an odd mix-

An ice cream in the morning...

The Historical Museum

ture of romanticism, classicism and functionalism, and cannot be called beautiful. But few would deny that the front steps in Fridtjof Nansens Plass on the side away from the sea are impressive, with the swan fountain and a huge cascade of water. On both sides of the courtyard is the **Yggdrasil Frieze**, carved in wood and illustrating themes from Norse mythology. Inside, light, and colour suffuse an airy central hall filled with frescoes and paintings.

It is but a short walk up from Fridtjof Nansens Plass back to Karl Johans Gate and towards the Palace. Turn right into Frederiksgate and head for the **Historical Museum**, which is part of the University. It consists of three departments – the **Ethnographical Museum**, the **Numismatic Collection** and the **Collection of Antiquities**. The **Viking Hall** gives the background to the discovery of the three ships which are now on display at Bygdøy; the Treasury holds beautiful articles in gold and silver; the Middle Ages collection predates the paintings in the National Gallery and is Oslo's richest collection of art up to 1530.

From here it is only a step across Halfdan Kjerulfs Plass into St Olavs Gate, then right to the **Museum of Applied Art** which houses the 13th-century Baldishol Tapestry, found at Nes in 1879.

8. Afternoon Shopping

Compared with much of Europe, Oslo came late to building temples to consumerism. But shopping under a glass roof has great benefits in a northern climate and the city has plunged into shopping centres in a big way, mostly in the area called Vaterland, just north of Jernbanetorget, near Oslo M, the new bus station.

The biggest shopping centre is **Oslo City**, at Stenersgate, all glass and sparkling white marble. The shops stay open until 8pm during the week and 6pm on Saturday. **Aker Brygge** down by the harbour is similar but places greater emphasis on eating, drinking and entertainment. **Paleet**, which opens on to Karl Johans Gate, opposite Studenterlunden, is one of the most elegant centres. Many people, however, find it preferable to browse along old city streets searching out the specialist shops.

Aker Brygge shopping-centre

Nostalgic settlement of accounts

Oslo's biggest and most comprehensive department store is **Steen & Strøm** (Kongensgate 23), near the Jernbanetorget end of Karl Johans Gate. **Glas Magasinet** in Stortorvet emphasises glass, china and pewter, always good in Norway. The ground-floor tourist shop sells ceramics and other craft work and hand-knitted Norwegian sweaters.

Norwegian chocolate is a dream. **Freia** is one of the best-known makes, and the company has a in Karl Johans gate. **David Andersen** jewellery is among the best known in Norway and also has its own shop (Karl Johans Gate 20). Near the City Hall, **Heyerdahl** (Fridtjof Nansens Plass 6) has a lovely selection of Norwegian silver, gold, pewter, enamel, and precious stones.

Grensen and **Lille Grensen** are happy hunting grounds for bargains, particularly on the latter's outdoor stalls, and **Youngstorvet**, as well as **Stortorvet**, has a daily market where the air round the stalls is sweet with the smell of flowers. For antiques, try the best, biggest and most expensive, **Kaare Berntsen** in Universitetsgaten 12, opposite the National Gallery. For something cheaper but interesting try **Antik-Bruktmarkedet**, (Trondheimsveien 13), a 15-minute walk up Storgata from the north side of the Domkirke. **Husfliden** is the largest stockist of Norwegian craftwork, from furniture to toys and *bunader* (national costumes) to kitchenware.

Similar collections are to be found in **Maurtua**, Fridtjof Nansens Plass 9, **William Schmidt** in Karl Johans Gate 41; and **Norway Designs** in Stortingsgaten 28, opposite the National Theatre.

Modern architecture at Aker Brygge

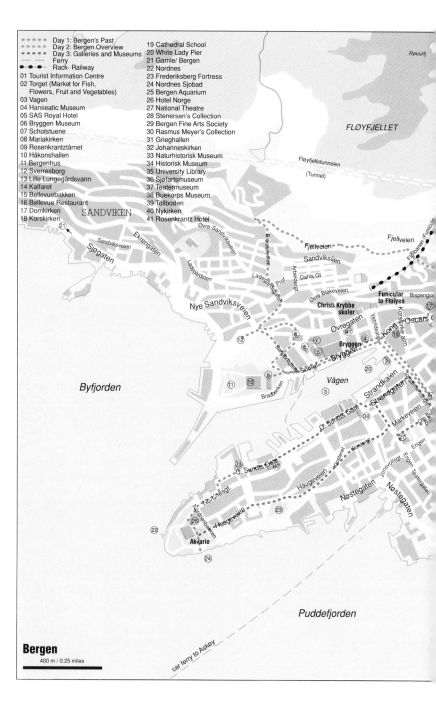

Day 1: Bergen's Past
Day 2: Bergen Overview
Day 3: Galleries and Museums
Ferry
Rack- Railway

01 Tourist Information Centre
02 Torget (Market for Fish,
   Flowers, Fruit and Vegetables)
03 Vågen
04 Hanseatic Museum
05 SAS Royal Hotel
06 Bryggen Museum
07 Schotstuene
08 Mariakirken
09 Rosenkrantztårnet
10 Håkonshallen
11 Bergenhus
12 Sverresborg
13 Lille Lungegårdsvann
14 Kalfaret
15 Bellevuebakken
16 Bellevue Restaurant
17 Domkirken
18 Korskirken

19 Cathedral School
20 White Lady Pier
21 Gamle/ Bergen
22 Nordnes
23 Frederiksberg Fortress
24 Nordnes Sjobad
25 Bergen Aquarium
26 Hotel Norge
27 National Theatre
28 Stenersen's Collection
29 Bergen Fine Arts Society
30 Rasmus Meyer's Collection
31 Grieghallen
32 Johanneskirken
33 Naturhistorisk Museum
34 Historisk Museum
35 University Library
36 Sjøfartsmuseum
37 Teatermuseum
38 Buekorps Museum
39 Tollboden
40 Nykirken
41 Rosenkrantz Hotel

SANDVIKEN

FLØYFJELLET

Fløyfjellstunnelen

(Tunnel)

Revurtj

Øvre Sandviksveien

Fjellveien

Sandviksveien

Sjøgaten

Ekregaten

Ladegårdsterr

Ladegårdsbakken

Breistreheien

Prof. Dahls Gt.

Øvre Blekeveien

Fjellveien

Sandvikslien

Christi Krybbe
skoler

Funicular
to Floiyen

Bispengs

Fløibanen Funicula

Nye Sandviksveien

Byfjorden

Øvregaten

Kong Oscars

Oscars

Korskirke alm

Veltesand

Bryggen

Bryggen

Vågen

Strandkaien

Strandgaten

Strandgaten

Markeveien

Bradbenken

Sandbrualm. Skjuset

C. Sundts Gate

Engen

Teatergaten

Engen

Nøstegaten

Nøstegaten

Jonsvollsgt.

Klostergt.

Klostergt.

C. Sundts Gate

Haugeveien

Kroneset.

Nordnesbakken

Haugeveien

Akvarie

Puddefjorden

car ferry to Askøy

Bergen

400 m / 0.25 miles

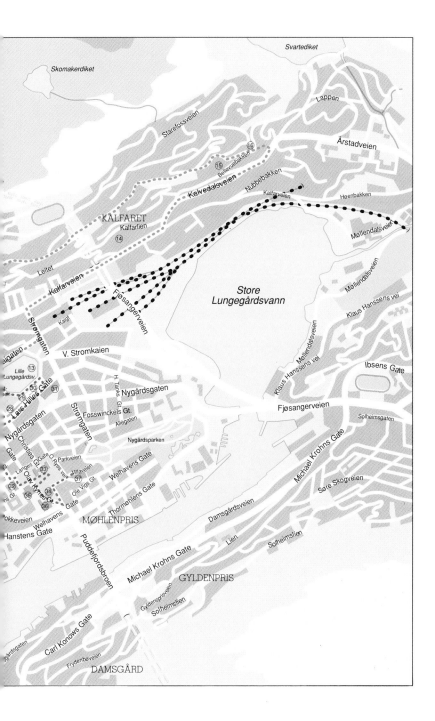

The heart of Bergen is Torget, the harbour square, where King Olav Kyrre founded his city in the 11th century. Today it holds the daily fish, flower and fruit market. Along the wharf, huddling close to the castle for protection, the medieval town grew and became the first capital of a united Norway and its biggest city until the 20th century when it was overtaken by Oslo. Bergen today has the natural layout and charm of a community built on hills. Almost all the itineraries and options on the following pages are based on public transport or walking. Make sure you have a comfortable pair of shoes for an energetic day. Bergen's rain is a national (though not necessarily always justified) joke and it has to be said that, when it does rain, the skies empty.

Bergen Tourist Board is a lively, helpful organisation which is working very hard to give good service to visitors and produces the invaluable *Bergen Guide*. I have found *Round Bergen on Foot* and *Skulpturer i Bergen* (Sculpture in Bergen), which describes some of the city's many sculptures, add interest to exploring. Ask in bookshops. Museums are mostly closed on Monday, and shut their doors at 3 or 4pm in the summer months (earlier in winter). Ask also about *Bybilletten*, a card given to visitors staying in certain hotels under the 'Bergen Weekend' scheme, which gives reductions on many tickets for theatres, concerts, parking and some travel.

1. Bergen's Past

From the Vågen fish market to Bryggen, the old part of the city, the Bryggen museums and the Mariakirken. To Fiskekrogen for lunch. In the afternoon to Rosenkrantztårnet and Håkonshallen Bergen's castles. Dinner at Enhjøringen on Bryggen.

On the way to **Vågen**, the old harbour at the edge of **Torget** with its fish, flower and fruit market, detour long enough to visit the **Tourist Information Office** (Tel: 32-14-80) in the centre of **Torgalmenningen**, a nearby pedestrian square, to pick up leaflets and maps, and make enquiries about tours.

   Bergen's fish market is awake early, and popular with locals and visitors alike. It dates back to the 16th century and today it is

What's on offer at the fish market

Old merchant's house in Bergen

bright with flowers and fruit as well as fish, gleaming silver as the boats unload their overnight catches, or laid out in glistening heaps on the stalls. You can buy smoked salmon rolls relatively cheaply and keep them for a snack lunch, or neat salmon packages to take home at the end of your visit. Notice the three flag poles guarded by stone lions which mark out a triangle that was once a ceremonial quay. A little way further out is the beautiful sailing ship *Statsraad Lehmkuhl*, now a sail training ship, also hired out for special occasions. On the right towards the sea, take note of **Zachariasbryggen**, an old warehouse, now largely reconstructed, with shops, offices, and cafés. This houses Fiskekrogen, your target for lunch, with summer tables outside serving beer and sandwiches.

Bryggen, on the east side of Vågen, is the oldest part of the city, where a line of medieval houses once clustered close to the water. King Olav Kyrre founded Bergen, but the walk along Bryggen is in fact more revealing of its medieval German past, when the Hanseatic traders dominated commerce along the Norwegian coast and Bergen was at the height of its power. The great fire of 1702 destroyed many Bryggen buildings but most were rebuilt and these Hanseatic houses are now on UNESCO's World Heritage list.

To keep your chronology correct, for the moment walk past these colourful buildings – just peeping sideways up the narrow wood-paved 'closes' that housed Bergen's early inhabitants – to **Bryggen Museum** (Tel: 31-67-10), near the **SAS Royal Hotel**. The museum

Tracteursted

had its birth in another of Bergen's catastrophic fires, in 1955, which led to the excavation of many archaeological treasures (some from the 12th century – sensitive reconstructions illustrate the life of that time). The SAS Royal Hotel also rose from the ashes of the 1955 fire when the architect, Oivind Maurseth, rebuilt six of the warehouse frontages, using original materials to do so.

Bryggen guides (often students) wear national costume for a tour that lasts around 1–1½ hours and includes Bryggen, the **Hanseatic Museum** (Tel: 31-41-89), and **Schøtstuene** (Tel: 31-60-20). Parties are then led back through Bryggen's maze of lanes and wooden tenements, many of which have come to life again as shops, workshops and restaurants. Here you will find **Bryggen Tracteursted** (Tel: 31-40-46), a 300-year-old inn which claims to be the oldest in Norway. Bryggen is the place to try out Bergen's specialities, such as *skillingsboller*, saucer-sized biscuit-buns flavoured with different spices. A single *bolle* with a coffee is sustenance enough for a quick midday snack.

The Hanseatic Museum is housed in one of the oldest and best preserved merchant houses where merchants and apprentices once gathered in the big communal room, with its enormous beer jug and a dried Royal Cod (distinguished by a knob on its forehead) hanging above. So great was the fear of fire that not a single stove was allowed in these tall wooden houses even during the excruciating cold of a Bergen winter. The only relief for merchant and apprentice alike was Schøtstuene, the German assembly rooms in **Ovregaten**, Bergen's oldest street. In this centre of German social life, a fire was permitted, the beer flowed, and the apprentices had their school lessons.

You are now almost back at Bryggens Museum and nearby is **Mariakirken** (St Mary's Church), Bergen's oldest functioning building. It dates from the 12th century, when the city was a centre of religious life with a cathedral and 20 churches. Mariakirken survived fires and war, has been altered and enlarged, and its finest treasure is the rich baroque pulpit, a German gift after Mariakirken became the Hanseatic League's church. The 15th-century Gothic triptych was probably made in Lübeck, and German was used for services until the 1920s.

Back at Vågen, **Fiskekrogen** (Tel: 31-75-66) specialises in fish and game and, remembering that no Norwegian restaurant meal is cheap, this is good value. Down by the harbour, sit outside for a beer (also not cheap) and then move into the small restaurant. If you have the stomach for it, the fish tank in the centre, watched

Inside the Mariakirken

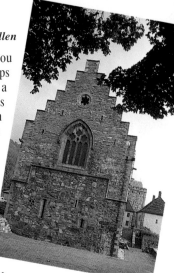

over by a large stuffed bear, allows you to make your own choice. Fish soups are excellent (around 50–60NKR) and a main course varies from crayfish tails with saffron sauce to a *sautå* of salmon and shellfish which will cost between 150–210NKR.

After lunch head north again past the German wharfhouses. Take a quick look at the angular red brick building on the corner, which is Bergen's **Kjøttbasar** (meat market), built in 1876. Notice too the unicorn's head standing out from the first storey above the bar **Sjø-boden**. Unicorn translates into the Norwegian **Enhjøringen**, the name of the restaurant for tonight's evening meal (Tel: 32-79-19). If you haven't already booked, it might be an idea to pop up the stairs now, for Bryggen as a whole is popular at night, and Enhjøringen's reputation is high.

Past the SAS Royal Hotel, the first tall building is **Rosenkrantz-tårnet** in what was known first as Holmen, later Bergenhus, where the city had its beginnings. From the 12th century, this fortified

Peace and tranquillity

area held the Royal Palace and military headquarters, and was also the centre of West Norway's religious life. In the 13th century, under King Håkon Håkonsson, Bergen became the capital of Norway and **Håkonshallen**, which you see next, was finished in 1261 for the coronation of Magnus Lagabøter (Lawmender). Rosenkrantztårnet – named after Erik Rosenkrantz, the Danish governor of Bergen in the 1560s – was built by stonemasons brought over from Scotland, which is why it looks very similar to a fortified Scottish house of the same period. The middle building between the tower and Håkonshallen is **Kommandantboligen** (the Commandant's Residence) built in 1725 and now the official residence of Western Norway's military chief of staff; the interior is not open to the public.

In 1944, when Bergen was occupied by German troops, an explosion in Vågen caused terrible damage, but this provided the opportunity to restore the buildings of Bergenhus as closely as possible to their original forms. Now, Håkonshallen has a beautiful banqueting and concert hall and Rosenkrantztårnet's medieval floors have been re-created.

Fish specialities

Though the walk back to the centre is short, you can pick up bus No 1 or 9 to the centre (**Torgalmenningen** or **Galleriet**), to rest and change at the hotel ready for the evening. **Enhjøringen**, which you passed earlier in Bryggen, was first mentioned in court evidence in 1304 by which time the German merchant, Herman Skult, had already lived there for 50 years; after the great fire of 1702, the house was rebuilt on its original foundations. Clamber up into the little series of rooms that form the restaurant, with its red beams, old furniture, and warm old-fashioned atmosphere.

Not surprisingly, Bergen is famous for its fish and seafood and Enhjørningen is a seafood restaurant. Try *gravet laks*, a cured salmon, with dill to start. Scandinavians are also caviar enthusiasts, and a *kaviar trio*, three types of caviar with raw onion and fresh cream, is also good. The servings here are huge and, though a shellfish dish may cost over 200NKR, it would serve three. Beer goes best with most Norwegian food, which is as well because wine is expensive. Enhjøringen's sister restaurant, **To Kokker** (Two Cooks; Tel: 32-28-16), is nearby and detailed in *Practical Information*.

For authentic pub life at the end of the meal, go below to **Sjøboden** for a final drink. It is usually full of seamen and oil workers and can be very noisy on Friday and Saturday nights.

2. Bergen Overview

Start at Torgalmenningen, the shopping centre, and catch the Bergen Express for its circular tour. To the Domkirken (Cathedral), before lunch at Kafe Augustus in the Galleriet shopping centre. The White Lady harbour cruise occupies the afternoon. Dinner in the Bellevue Restaurant.

The Bergen Express

Patrolling Bryggen

Begin the day at the Tourist Information Centre to book tickets for the **White Lady harbour cruise** at 2.30pm which leaves from the left-hand quay of the Fish Market you can also book at the kiosk there), and enquire if the **Buekorps Museum** will be open on the following day. Either here or in your hotel, enquire about **Fana Folklore** for the following evening.

At **Torgalmenningen** you are at the heart of Bergen's shopping centre, which extends left into **Strandgaten**. For later reference, take a quick look at the windows of **Sundt**, one of Bergen's biggest department stores, and the entrance to the shopping centre **Galleriet**, for lunch time. You can scarcely miss the national monument to seamen, a granite and bronze block which commemorates Norway's seafaring achievements from Viking times to the 20th century, with figures illustrating the Norsemen's 11th-century voyage to North America, the Norwegian voyages to Greenland, merchant ships and whaling, and finally Norway's 20th-century oil transport.

At 10am, the **Bergen Express**, a little red-painted road train, takes off from a stop near the Information Centre. The train moves along beside the town lake, **Lille Lungegårdsvann**, and then up **Kalfaret** to **Bellevuebakken** and the **Bellevue Restaurant** (Tel: 31-02-40), tonight's dining spot. The Bergen Express then puffs along **Fjellveien**, the mountain road, and through one of the city's most distinctive old districts. From here it is easy to appreciate how much Bergen is a city of fjord, lake and mountain. The journey wends down past Mulen to Mariakirken, through Bergenhus and back along Bryggen and Torget to the starting point. An alterna-

Picturesque streets

The Bergen Express

tive for this morning ride might be a shopping expedition, a light lunch, and taking the last Bergen Express (7pm) up to the restaurant for an early supper, which you should in any case book.

An hour later, back in the centre, cross the wide road from Torget and take **Kong Oscars Gate** to **Domkirken** (cathedral) the only medieval church apart from Mariakirken to survive Bergen's ferocious fires. Though much has had to be rebuilt, this part of Bergen echoes the medieval city in its layout and style and the whole area of small criss-cross streets and squares lends itself to wandering. On the way to Domkirken, you see **Korskirken** (Holy Cross Church) to the right but the church is rarely open. If you can get inside, there are fragments of the earliest church (1150) but Korskirken was damaged by fire so many times, even before the great fire of 1702, that the cross-shaped building is now a mixture of styles.

Domkirken also faced war and fire but Magnus Lagabøter rebuilt it in the late 13th century and much of his nave and choir remain. After the Reformation it became Bergen's Reformed Cathedral, but was again a casualty during the 1665 Battle of Vågen, when an English cannonball ploughed into the wall above the west door. If you can time your visit for a Thursday, the organist gives a short recital at noon, which adds immensely to the true atmosphere of this sturdy cathedral. Next door is the **Cathedral School**, always known as the Latin School, where the Norwegian-born playwright and poet, Ludvig Holberg (commemorated in Grieg's *Holberg Suite*) had his education, before gravitating to Copenhagen at a time when Denmark still ruled Norway.

Galleriet on the south side of Torgalmenningen is one of three relatively new shopping centres, ideal when winter snows hit the city. The basement floor is like a huge garden of plants, the faint scent drifting up to the galleries above. Shops here aim to attract both locals and visitors. A first class bookshop with a great many books in English indicates Norwegian linguistic prowess, a sports shop has the latest in brand names and the good quality leather and knitwear is popular with visitors, as is gold and silver jewellery

'Statsraad Lehmkuhl' lying at anchor

in the *gullsmed* (goldsmith) on the ground floor. **Kafe Augustus** (Tel: 32-32-25) is on the top gallery.

Kafe Augustus is owned by the **Augustin Hotel** on the waterfront to the east of Vågen and, as well as unusual soups, salads, hot and and cold dishes, has an excellent counter with cakes, pastries and the ubiquitous *smørbrød* (open sandwich) big enough for a light meal at a cost of 40NKR upwards. A glass of wine will set you back a minimum of 30NKR but Kafe Augustus makes a pleasant place to sit and watch the passers-by.

Before 2.30pm, you should be at the **White Lady pier** at the harbour square. The boat sets off past the fine rigging of the *Statsraad Lehmkuhl* towards the harbour mouth with the quays for ferries

Byfjorden

from Denmark, England, the Shetland and Faroe Islands; in summer they accommodate cruise ships. Eighty thousand people arrive in Bergen each year by these vessels. From a boat, it is easy to realise how much Bergen has depended upon the sea. The *White Lady* passes a continuous line of coloured wooden warehouses and fishing sheds, mostly still in use. The goal is a seaview of **Gamle Bergen** (Old Bergen) at **Elsesro**, an open-air museum where a group of 35 wooden houses from the 18th and 19th centuries are gathered (see Itinerary 5).

As the *White Lady* turns east across **Byfjorden**, Bergen's green islands begin to appear and at weekends the water is dotted with boats and sails. The island ahead, with the **Deep Sea**

The Bellevue restaurant

Diving School at the edge of the water, is **Askøy**. The ferry turns next into **Puddefjorden**, slips under a high bridge and passes the quay used by the coastal steamer (*Hurtigruten*) that leaves around 10pm each night for its 3,579km (2,224 mile) trip around Nordkap (North Cape) to Kirkenes on the Russian border and back. Heading for the **Nordnes Peninsula** (the eastern arm of Vågen) you get a glimpse of **Frederiksberg Fortress** and, below it, the popular **Nordnes Sjøbad** (bathing place) which also has a heated outdoor pool. At the tip of Nordnes Peninsula is the **Bergen Aquarium**.

In the evening, if you plan to go to the **Bellevue Restaurant** by Bergen Express, catch the last one from Torgalmenningen at 7pm. Bus No 11 from the Post Office (behind Galleriet) also goes to the restaurant and runs till midnight. In the long, light evening, the Bellevue Restaurant provides the day's final views of Bergen from wide windows which look down like the bridge of a great ship. Before it opened as a restaurant in 1899, this was the family home of the Saudan family. The set lunch menu starts at around 160NKR but dinner with wine, is likely to cost 500NKR per head.

3. Galleries and Museums

A day which includes visits to the National Theatre, Stenersen's Collection, Rasmus Meyer's Collection, Grieghallen, Johanneskirken, Naturhistorisk Museum, Sjøfartsmuseum and others. Lunch in the Lido Café. After lunch, via the Buekorps Museum to Nordnes Point, Aquarium and swimming pool. Evening: Fana Folklore (book through the hotel or Tourist Information Office).

Start off from **Ole Bulls Plass** beside **Hotel Norge**, and just up the hill from Torgalmenningen. On the right is the **National Theatre**, an art nouveau building which opened in 1909. Most productions are in Norwegian but, during the **Bergen International Festival** (music and drama) in the spring, you might find something in English. Ole Bull founded the theatre in 1850 (in a building destroyed during World War II) and the statue on the west side is of the nationalist and writer Bjørnstjerne Bjørnson, who was for a time director of the theatre and wrote the words for the Norwegian National Anthem.

The Grieghallen

Colour contrast on the Johanneskirken

Return to Ole Bulls Plass and Hotel Norge and walk east towards the town park and Lille Lungegårdsvann, past the music pavilion where brass bands, very popular in Norway, play in the summer. Close by is a statue of the composer Edvard Grieg. Cross over **Christies Gate** and into the park. On the right of the lake three adjoining buildings hold the art collections but, if you plan to visit the museums, do not try to tackle them all in one morning.

The first two buildings house the **Stenersen's Collection** (Tel: 97-80-00), and **Bergen Fine Arts Society**'s gallery (Tel: 32-14-60). The Picassos and Klees of the Stenersen's Collection form a blazing contrast to Norway's most famous European painter, Edvard Munch, also well represented. The Fine Arts Society contains Norwegian paintings from the last 150 years; it is open throughout the year with changing exhibitions of contemporary art. **Rasmus Meyer's Collection** (Tel: 97-80-00), in the next building, again features Norwegian artists such as J C Dahl, born in Bergen, and Harriet Backer, and holds many Munch works.

Leaving Meyer's collection, turn right to face **Grieghallen**, opened in 1978. Shaped like a grand piano, this unusual hall has contributed enormously to the success of the Bergen International Festival, and its acoustics are superb. It is the home of Norway's oldest orchestra, the Bergen Philharmonic, founded in 1765, which performs every Thursday from September to June. Follow **Lars Hilles Gate**, back across Christies Gate until you meet Torggaten. Turn left here and begin the long climb up cobbles and steps with the unmistakable red brick façade and green copper steeple of **Johanneskirken** ahead. This area, known as **Nygårdshøyden**, was built at the end of the last century to house the rich Bergensere. It is still the university area, with a cluster of museums, though many of the newer faculties have now moved further out.

Take the diagonal path left across the grass beside the church for the **Naturhistorisk Museum**, a magnificent building from the end of the last century; known simply as 'The Museum', it is the kernel of

Tête-à-tête in the aquarium

the university. Once this area was called Hangman's Hill and it was the town's place of execution. Today, the peaceful gardens around the museum are the University Botanic Garden. At the far side, the **Historisk Museum** covers art, culture, archaeology and ethnology. A tunnel at the foot of the museum's tower goes through the hill and is still used as a short cut into the **Møhlenpris** area.

To the right of the Historisk Museum are two later buildings, the **University Library** and Bergen's **Sjøfartsmuseum** (Maritime Museum; Tel: 32-79-80), both opened in the early 1960s. The last is probably the most evocative of this seafaring area and the exhibits range from Old Norse times to the present. Not far from the Historisk Museum on the other side is the **Teatermuseum** on **Villaveien**, the street which preserves some of Bergen's magnificent 19th-century villas. After the stiff climb up, you may be thankful to walk back down for lunch. **Lido Café and Restaurant** (Tel: 32-59-12) is at Torget, with a view of the fish market.

After lunch, walk along Strandgaten from Torgalmenningen to a small, square building, a bit like an old gatehouse, called **Muren**. The ground floor holds little shops and the first floor was once a banqueting hall, now the **Buekorps Museum**. This private museum is rarely open, but in summer you can hardly miss the Buekorps, whose history goes back some 135 years. It is something like a boys' brigade; its members wear a distinctive uniform, and today still play their part in many local celebrations.

From here, Strandgaten becomes a pedestrian street. Turn left till you reach **Klostergaten** and walk along towards **Nordnes Point**. The area is a maze of old buildings and narrow lanes such as **Knøsesmauet**, which plunges steeply down between wooden buildings. The tower at the top was once a guardhouse, built in 1774. Further on, along Strangehagen and Galgebakken, is **Frederiksberg**, part of the 17th-century defensive walls.

Bergen's **Aquarium** has one of Europe's best collections of seals and penguins. Near here, try out another of Bergen's bathing places, **Nordnes Sjøbad**, with a heated outdoor pool. Afterwards, you can pick up the No 4 bus back, but the walk is only 15 min-

The young generation of folk dancers

utes and, if you return via the Vågen side of the peninsula, you pass **Tollboden**, (the Customs House) a beautiful building from 1744 which, though badly damaged by a 1944 explosion, has been fully restored. Further on is **Nykirken** (New Church), which belies its name – there has been a church here since the Middle Ages. It was last rebuilt in 1956 and its beautiful galleries can be seen by going in through the door to the rear. From here, it is but a step along the pedestrian street to the Buekorps Museum, and thence, via Wackendorffsgaten and Trånplassen, which holds the **Bergen Court House**, back to Torgalmenningen.

Tonight, go to **Fana Folklore** (book ahead) a traditional Norwegian evening designed as a country wedding. The main season is from June until the end of August but Fana Folklore is also open on some evenings during May and September. Buses leave **Festplassen** (across Christies Gate from the bandstand) at 7pm on Monday, Tuesday, Thursday and Friday for the half-hour journey to the old **Fanakirke** south-west of the city for a short recital of traditional tunes. You then go on to **Rambergstunet** (an old farm) to be greeted by a fanfare on the *lur*, an ancient musical instrument a bit like a coaching horn. Guests sit at long wooden tables, with a view of the **Fana Fjord**, and the food, music, dancing, and singing begins. The brilliant costumes and the traditional dancing, to lively airs played on an old fiddle, give the evening an authentic warmth.

An alternative to this colourful evening is the Monday and Wednesday folklore programme given by the **Bjørgvin Regional Folk-dancing Group** in Bryggens Museum. The performances start at 8.30pm and, if you prefer to eat beforehand, many hotels have a tourist menu served up to 7pm. Near at hand, for example, the **Rosenkrantz Hotel** (Tel: 31-50-00) in Rosenkrantzgate, just behind Bryggen, is a good bet at around 90NKR for one course and coffee.

4. Grieg's Troldhaugen

A morning or afternoon spent at Grieg's home at Troldhaugen and at Fantoft Stavkirke (church).

For the last 20 years of his life, Norway's most famous composer, Edvard Grieg, spent his summers at **Troldhaugen**, the elegant wooden house he built on a promontory above the peace of **Nordås Lake**, just off the E68 in the direction of **Fana** (south-west). By the water is the writing *hytte* (hut) where he composed many of his best-known works. He was buried there and you can see his gravestone and that of his wife, the singer Nina Hagerup.

Inside Troldhaugen

Grieg was very much part of the 19th-century flood of nationalism that swept Norway. Born in Bergen in 1843, he was descended from a Scottish merchant, Alexander Greig, who emigrated from Aberdeen to Bergen in 1779. The composer was much influenced by Norwegian folk music and he and the violinist Ole Bull spent many weeks each year trekking the great mountain massifs of Jotunheimen and Hardangervidda, transcribing traditional folk songs. Another product of these ecpeditions is his incidental music to Henrik Ibsen's *Peer Gynt*, based on stories from Vinstra, in Eastern Norway.

Troldhaugen is preserved as Grieg left it, with his armchair, manuscripts, books, and piano, still in working order. In summer, recitals and concerts are held in the house although most take place in **Troldsalen**, a hall in the grounds which holds 200 people. On the way back to Bergen, visit **Fantoft Stave Church** in the district of Paradis. (A village on the rail line north of Trondheim has the name of Hell, which makes train tickets collector's items!)

Outside Troldhaugen

Nothing is more Norwegian than the *stavkirke* (stave churches) which get their name from their solid, upright timber trunks. With their roofs shaped like the curves of a Viking ship, these are the churches of people hankering after their pagan past. Fantoft is one of the 12th-century buildings whose strength and structural ingenuity has kept them standing for 700 years. Many such churches were destroyed during the 19th century and today only 28 remain in Norway. In its original home at Fortun, at the head of the Sognefjord, Fantoft Stavkirke might have suffered the same fate. But when, in 1879, the village decided to build a new church, a far sighted Bergenser, Konsul F Gade, bought it and had it dismantled and brought to Bergen.

Troldhaugen and Fantoft are easily reached by car but awkward by bus and foot. The simplest alternative is one of the tours that leave from, and return to, the side of the **Hotel Norge**. At 10.30am, **De Gule Bussene** (the yellow buses) leave for a three-hour tour, and at 3.30pm the **Unitur** bus leaves from the same place. The price for either is 125NKR and includes a guide. (Book at the Norge, the Tourist Information Centre or simply chance a place on the bus.) Before or after, Hotel Norge's **Ole Bull Restaurant** (Tel: 21-01-00) offers an excellent *koldtbord* from noon until 6pm.

The Fantoft Stavkirke

5. Gamle Bergen

An afternoon by bus or car to Gamle Bergen, at Elsesro.

Bergen has long been renowned for the beauty of its wooden houses and, despite many fierce fires, a surprising number remain. **Gamle Bergen** (Old Bergen) is an attempt to show what Bergen must have been like in the 18th and 19th centuries by recreating a small West Norwegian community of 35 houses brought in from various places to the old estate of Elsesro. To reach Gamle Bergen takes no more than 15 minutes on bus No 1 or 9 from the centre (behind the Post Office) or by car north-west on road 14.

The houses range across the social spectrum from the tiny **Sypikenshus** (the Seamstress's House), just a room and kitchen where she lived and plied her needle, to the grand ballroom of **Embetsmannshuset** (the Official's Residence) with French imperial-style wallpaper made in Paris in 1824 showing a Greek festival. **Barbersalongen** (the Barber's Shop), with heavy, padded seats and a comfortable masculine air was the place where the men met. It is full of 19th-century barbers' equipment, and **Kjøpmannshuset** (the Merchant's House) has much of the same comfort, particularly in the living room with its potted plants and stuffed sofas.

From a slightly earlier period, **Krohnstedet** is a wealthy country house, dated 1785, decorated for a party on 20 June 1808 and preserved in aspic at Gamle Bergen. When Louis Daguerre displayed his historic first photograph in Paris in 1839, The Bergensere enthused and by 1852 the city had its own photographer. At Gamle Bergen, the **Photographer's Studio** dates from around the turn of the century and is full of fascinating contem-

porary equipment. But most tempting of all is the aroma from **Bakerhuset** (the Baker's House), once situated just off Bryggen near Mariakirken. When the bakery is preparing the traditional pastries which are on sale in the Museum, the smells of the wood-fired stove and of the traditional recipes mingle temptingly.

The main estate building still stands in its original place and has a restaurant open from noon–7pm, May to September. The last tour is 6pm (in summer, earlier at other times) but if you are this late at Gamle Bergen, you might choose to eat early in the restaurant before the tour. Another alternative is to wander down towards the sea to swim at **Sandviken Sjøbad**, one of Bergen's best bathing places. Sea bathing in these sheltered waters, even this far north, is amazingly warm at the height of summer.

6. Fløien

By funicular to Fløien, Bergen's spectacular 'mountain'.

Make sure you have the Information Centre's leaflet and sketch map of **Fløien**, *Gledes Kartet,* before you walk across to **Fløibanen's** bottom station on the far side of Torget and up past the Meat Market. Here the little funicular railway whisks up 320m (1,000ft) to the top station in something under eight minutes. Try to get into the lowest carriage for the most spectacular view of the Bergen panorama. On the return, sit here only if you have a head for heights though there is no need to be nervous. Fløibanen, Scandinavia's first cable railway, has been climbing smoothly up and down the mountain since 1918 without an accident.

From the top station, where there is a small coffee bar and shop, Bergen below is a map of islands and peninsulas which lead gradually towards the North Sea. Seven protective hills shelter the city: Blåmanen, Rundemanen Sandviksfjellet and the distant Storsåta to the north, Damsgårdfjellet, Løvstakken to the west and Ulriken, to the south, at 642m (2,105ft) the highest of the seven, with its own cable car up to a top station and restaurant.

Fløien, with its summer restaurant in

a beautiful 1925 building nearby (now used by the School of Architecture), is Bergen's nearest open hill country, where people ski in winter and walk in summer. There are some 25km (15 miles) of track, all colour-coded to the sketch map. It is typical West Norwegian hill country, woods, heath, peak and lake. One of the most pleasant and easiest walks is the track around **Skomakerdiket**, a popular bathing lake; for the more energetic, the track past **Brushytten** leads up to **Blåmanen**, some 552m (1,700ft) above a lake **Blåmansvannet**. None of the walks is more than 5km (3 miles). In summer, **Fløien Restaurant** is a peaceful setting for a leisurely coffee or lunch on the verandah, and for shelter when it is wet.

It can be fun to walk down or, less energetic but nonetheless interesting, try taking the train to the **Fjellveien** station above the terminal, and stroll through **Fjellien** where the white wooden houses and cobbles have changed their character very little over many years. At the foot of the hill in Ovregaten is Bergen's oldest school, **Christi Krybbe** (Christ in the Crib), a primary school since 1740, and at No 17 you come to **GlasHuset**, which has been making and selling glass for over 40 years.

View of Bergen

UNDTUR-EXCURS...
GE I ET NØTESKALL NORWAY IN A NUTSHE
EN · FLÅM · GUDVANGEN · STALHEIM · VOSS · BERGEN
e nr 877
GEN · FLÅM · GUDVANGEN · STALHEIM · VOSS · BERGEN
eller omvendt or vice versa

1. Norway in a Nutshell

The steepest, narrowest, highest, fiercest, longest, most beautiful scenery in Norway.

This West Norwegian itinerary gives you not only the scenery for which Norway has become justly famous but also a taste of the varied and comprehensive transport system that is needed in such a vast, mountainous country. In summer, the tour starts by train from Bergen around 10am it soon plunges into a tunnel, then bursts out again to reach the tranquil **Sørfjorden**, and winds its way along the fjord towards **Stanghella**.

The train then turns north-east through **Dale** and follows the water almost to **Voss**, centre of a rich farming district. After passing Voss (there is a short stop there on the way back) the train enters the longest tunnel on this part of the line, the 5km (3 mile) **Gravhals Tunnel**. At Myrdal, you change to a small train for

Stone church in Voss

Flåm, nearly 850m (2,800ft) below, down **Flåmsdalen** to the edge of **Aurlandsfjorden**, one of the innermost finger tips of **Sognefjord**, more than 156km (97 miles) from the sea. The Flåm line is a miracle of engineering, snaking 6km (4 miles) down the narrow mountain valley, through 20 tunnels and flickering in and out of winter snow screens. The gradient is the steepest in Europe used by a conventional train. **Kjosfossen** waterfall is at its most magnificent in May, and you get another chance to see the cascading waters jumping from ledge to ledge through the dark walls of a ravine between Kjosfossen and the Bakli tunnel.

This itinerary allows enough time for lunch at Flåm, which is served at the **Fretheim Hotel** (Tel: 056-32-200, not included in the ticket), before taking the ferry which moves gently up Aurlands-fjorden at the start of a two-hour voyage to **Gudvangen**. On both sides, mountains swoop into the water and every tiny water meadow has space for a small farm or a cluster of wooden houses. The biggest community along this fjord is **Aurland**, famous for its shoes. The ferry turns south-west into **Nærøyfjorden**, the narrowest in Europe, where the height of the mountains is double the width of the fjord. The next stop is Gudvangen, dwarfed by precipitous mountains, and from here the tour continues by bus into **Nærøy-dalen**, past the entrance to the new tunnel from Gudvangen to **Landhuso** which will make it possible to make the whole journey by road. From the hairpin bends of the road up **Stalheimskleiven** (gorge) you can see two fine waterfalls, **Stalheimfossen** and **Sivle-fossen**, named after the Norwegian poet Per Sivle, whose child-hood home stands above.

During World War II, the Stalheim Gorge was the scene of fierce fighting when Norwegian forces held out at the **Stalheim Hotel**, the highest point. Stalheim has been a coaching inn since the 17th century and the bus makes a welcome brief stop at the present ho-tel which is an excellent place to buy souvenirs. At Voss there is no time for exploration, just a quick coffee before the train leaves for Bergen; it arrives back in the city at around 8pm.

Nature's tranquillity

2. Lysøen

A cultural and musical day on Ole Bull's island of Lysøen.

Lysøen, the last home of Norway's famed 19th-century violinist, Ole Bull, lies some 30km (19 miles) south-west of Bergen. This beautiful island in **Lysefjorden** has been inhabited since the Middle Ages, when it belonged to the monks of Lysekloster on the mainland. The ruins of their community can be visited if you have time.

Take bus No 127 or 128 (for **Dragna**) from platform 20 at Bergen bus station, and ask the driver to set you down at **Buena Kai** for the boat to Lysøen. By car, take roads 14 or E68 out to **Nestun**, then follow signs to **Fana**, and the hill road over Fanafjell to the **Sørestraumen** crossroads. Turn right down to Buena Kai and Lysøen will be hard to miss. The Ole Bull ferry leaves for the island on the hour from noon–3pm, returning at 10 minutes to the hour up to 3.50pm (Sunday 11am–4.50pm). Sailings allow some three hours on the island, time enough to take the guided tour of the house and explore some of the paths which Bull constructed through natural woodland.

Opposite and right: Ole Bull's house

The house is an astonishing building with a strange onion dome tower. Bull called it his 'Little Alhambra'. He built it for his second wife, the American Sara Thorp, and the design was largely his own. It includes a recital room, seating 120. Inside, the house is Norwegian pine but every room is a mixture of styles, flamboyant carvings and decoration. One of Ole Bull's violins is on display here, but his greatest one is on show in West Norway's Museum of Applied Arts in Bergen. The music room is a rich cavern showing the influences of Bull's travels. There is also a highly unsuccessful piano designed by Bull, which he turned into a solid desk.

The house is full of gifts from admirers: a tapestry in the bedroom made by ladies of the Russian court, an 80-stone diamond ring from the Czar. When Ole Bull died in 1880, 14 ships escorted his coffin to Bergen and 25–30,000 people attended his funeral. His wife and daughter continued to spend summers on Lysøen, as did his granddaughter, Sylvea Bull Curtis, who preserved the building and island until 1973, when she donated the estate to the Norwegian Society for the Preservation of Historical Monuments; they re-opened it as a museum in 1984. A bust of Sylvea Bull Curtis by Hans Jacob Meyer stands in the garden in front of the house.

Throughout the summer, and particularly during the **Bergen International Festival** (held in May and June), the old music room again resounds to the music that Bull played there, with violin recitals and small ensembles. Advance booking is necessary (Tel: 30-90-77), and the audience travels out from Bergen by special coach. This is an idyllic setting for listening to music.

Musical climax at the Bergen festival

Shopping

What to Buy

The first thing to remember is that Norwegian goods are high quality and often highly priced. That does not mean that they are not good value, particularly if you take advantage of the tax-free schemes with savings of 10–15 per cent. In the shop, you pay in full and collect a 'cheque' for the amount. The tax portion is refunded on the way out of the country from special tax-free representatives (not customs officers) at airports, ports, and frontiers.

Almost all Norway's museums and galleries have a shop which sells a variety of interesting and typical items. The most frequent souvenir is a **troll**, of every shape and degree of ugliness. Up in the mountains, surrounded by the weird outlines of rocks and trees, it is easy to understand how Norwegians came to believe in the mythology of the troll, unfriendly creatures which lived in the mountains and came out at night to do their mischief. Looking for something typical, I much prefer a piece of *rosemaling* (**rose-painting**) – delicately painted wooden plates and household items, in patterns particular to different areas.

Most children love **dolls** in the traditional *bunader* or national costumes, which also vary tremendously from region to region. Sami (Lapp) craftwork includes similar dolls in their distinctive costume. Authentic work is labelled *Sami Duodji*.

Traditional skills have often been adapted to modern

A troll keeps an eye on shoppers

designs. The decorated *bunad* includes beautiful metal **jewellery**, so it is no surprise that gold and silverwork is excellent in Norway. Norway also has a lot of minerals, precious and semi-precious **gemstones**, often used in designs, including a beautiful slightly-mottled pink stone that is a bit like the traditional Greenlandic *tutapit*. Enamelled silver jewellery is very striking. In the same way, the tradition of **wood carving** continues in the production of an attractive range of bowls and other utensils.

Norwegian **knitted jackets**, sweaters and socks are famous. Again, the patterns vary according to the region and knitters in Setersdal and Fana are reputed to be among the best. Like the *bunad*, Norwegian **sweaters** are durable enough to hand down to the next generation and the silver clasps are very beautiful. Occasionally new patterns appear and the one designed for Norway's Winter Olympic team by the Dale Knitwear Company is very popular.

Glass and porcelain are good buys, the former traditionally having a slightly grey tint, which is still seen in some modern glass. All three main glassworks at Hadeland, Magnor, and Randsfjorden welcome visitors to watch glass-blowing, and have retail shops.

Anyone who has visited the north of Norway knows that a **fur coat** is a way of keeping alive in winter. Norwegians excel at mak-

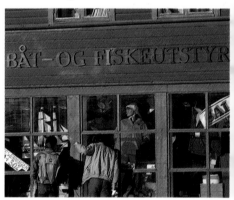

ing goods like this, which fit in with the way of life and climate. It is the same with **sport and outdoor equipment**, such as boots (not cheap) that really keep out the cold and wet. And nowhere will you find a better or more comfortable rucksack. One I purchased at a sale in Oslo, designed for schoolchildren's day-to-day use, is big enough for overnight necessities. This must indicate something about Norwegian schoolchildren! But if it is **food** you are after, take home a packet of the cured salmon, *gravet laks*, which gives a true flavour of Norway.

Hours

Shopping hours are usually 9am–4.30/5pm, though you will find variations, with late night on Thursday (sometimes also Friday) usually to 7pm, Saturday 9am–2pm. Many new shopping malls in Bergen and Oslo stay open longer, sometimes until 8pm on weekdays, 6pm on Saturday.

What to Eat

Once on a visit to Norway, I was served reindeer twice in one day. Though the timing was not the best, it was nevertheless a compliment, for reindeer is a Norwegian speciality, a meal for special days and special guests. As in other northern peasant societies,

Specialities=
Bergen Fish soup
Catfish
Reindeer
Salads

Norway's traditional cooking was, and in some senses still is, based on food that could be grown and raised in a short summer or taken from the sea, even at dangerous seasons, and preserved for harder times.

Dried, salted and smoked meats (*spekemat*) were a staple, along with dried, cured and pickled fish, particularly herring. Kept in a barrel in the corner of the kitchen for months on end, this was part of the regular diet. Butter- and cheese-making left milk residues that could also be turned into various foods. Today, this humble fare has graduated to being fine food and dried, cured and marinated fish and meat are still important ingredients in Norwegian cooking. Every hotel will offer a selection of specially prepared fish and cooked meat on the breakfast table as well as later in the day, and it is easy to acquire a taste for sour milk with cereals. This breakfast table will usually be graced with a particularly fruity jam, not as stiff and oversweet as some and also surprisingly good with cereals.

Fish, from cod and mackerel to trout and salmon, is excellent, and *fiskeboller* (fish balls in a béchamel sauce) are regulars on every family's menu, served along with the plain, boiled potatoes that appear with even greater regularity. A sprinkling of fresh dill and butter lifts them out of the everyday. Definitely special is salmon, fresh baked or boiled, smoked with a flavour that is particular to its area, or served as *gravet laks,* a speciality claimed by each Scandinavian country as its own. *Gravet laks* is an uncooked but cured salmon, quite different from, and much more interesting than, smoked salmon. It is served very thinly sliced with a dill or mustard-based sauce and sprigs of dill, which is also used during the curing. Shellfish, including crabs, lobster and prawns, are naturals for a country with a long fishing coast, and favourites for *smørbrød.*

Even today, Norwegian specialities are often prepared from ingredients preserved in old traditional ways. In many places, particularly on the west coast, *klippfisk* (split dried cod) is used for a variety of recipes, and sometimes adapted to the cuisines of other countries, for example a *klippfisk* version of *bacalao* is popular on

Specialities of Norwegian cuisine

certain parts of the west coast. A delicacy for the Norwegian palate, though foreigners rarely appreciate the chewy texture, is *lutefisk*. This is fish marinaded in *lye* (dictionary definition: 'a strong alkaline solution; a liquid used for washing') and distinctly an acquired taste. The *akvavit* (a grain- or potato-based spirit; often flavoured with caraway) or *øl* (beer) that goes with it helps novices to wash it down, but *lutefisk* is more something to try as a challenge than as a meal. *Akvavit*, perhaps chased with beer, is also good with the pickled herrings that start *Det store koldtbord*.

The *koldtbord*, the cold table, familiar throughout Scandinavia though each country has its own distinctive style, is far more than its name suggests. On high days and holidays – and often at lunchtime in hotels – it starts with varieties of herring, goes on through fish, shellfish, patés and cold meats and, despite the name, continues with hot dishes, followed by cheese and puddings. The correct way of eating is not to pile your plate but to return to the table, taking small quantities. *Det store koldtbord* is not a meal to be eaten in a hurry.

Norway has an abundance of berries in forest and hillside from late spring into autumn, and these are available in markets in season. Berry-picking is popular enough over a weekend to make Monday-morning stained fingers almost fashionable. Best of all to my taste is *multer,* a yellow-coloured berry that is akin to a cloud berry, but there are also *blåbær* (blueberries or blaeberries), and wild strawberries have a specially delicate taste. Try them all with sour cream.

The range of breads and pastries available is wide. *Flatbrød* is good with cheese, and dark-coloured rye bread makes the best base for the many stronger-tasting sandwich ingredients.

Eating out in Norway has never been cheap but over the last decade the range and style of restaurants has expanded enormously. Particularly in Oslo, Stavanger and Bergen, an influx of foreign restaurants has added to the choice; but it is wise to remember that these are not of the cheap Chinese or Indian 'carry-out' variety travellers will come across in many parts of the world. Even so, the prices can sometimes be competitive and if your funds are short you can always try *pølser*, a kind of hot dog, or *vaffler* (waffles) from a street kiosk, for really good value.

Recommendations

The following list includes restaurants already suggested under individual itineraries. A rough price guide for dinner per head without wine: *Inexpensive*: under 150NKR; *Moderate*: 150–300NKR; *Expensive*: 300–500-plus NKR. A quick and simple meal at lunch time should cost well below 100NKR.

Oslo

ANNEN ETAGE (HOTEL CONTINENTAL)
Stortingsgate 24–26. Tel: 41-90-60.
One of Norway's best known exclusive restaurants. *Expensive.*

ATRIUM (ROYAL CHRISTIANIA HOTEL)
Biskop Gunnerusgate. Tel: 42-94-10.
Very reasonably priced meal in superb atrium setting. *Moderate* to *Inexpensive* (lunch-time). Also gourmet restaurant. *Expensive.*

BRASSERIET (SAS HOTEL)
Holbergsgate 30. Tel: 11-30-00.
Good international cuisine with Norwegian specialities, particularly seafood. *Expensive.*

BRISTOL GRILL
Kristian IV's Gate 7. Tel: 41-58-40.
Superb midday *koldtbord* and evening meals in famous old hotel. Popular with Oslonians. *Expensive.*

DET GAMLE RAADHUSET
Nedre Slottsgate 1. Tel: 42-01-07.
Traditional food, particularly seafood, in one of Oslo's oldest buildings. See Oslo Itinerary 2. *Moderate.*

ENGEBRET CAFÉ
Bankplassen. Tel: 33-66-94.
Generous lunchtime *koldtbord* and à la carte at night. See Oslo Itinerary 2. *Moderate* to *Expensive* (but you can just have a pudding or gateau and cream with your coffee outside).

GAMLESTUA
In Steen & Strøm store. Tel: 41-68-00.
Traditional Norwegian food, good value. *Inexpensive.*

GRAND CAFÉ (GRAND HOTEL)
Karl Johans Gate 31. Tel: 42-93-90.
Ibsen's home ground. See Oslo Itinerary 3. *Moderate.*

LANTERNEN KRO
Kro Huk Aveny Bygdøy. Tel: 43-81-25.
Traditional inn and steakhouse at Dronningen. Indoor and outdoor. See Oslo Itinerary 3. *Moderate.*

HENRIKKE
Studenterlunden. Tel: 41-78-27.
Eat inside or outside. See Oslo Itinerary 1. *Inexpensive.*

HOLMENKOLLEN CAFETERIA
Holmenkollvn. 119. Tel: 14-62-26.
Below the ski jump tower with lovely view and outside terrace. *Inexpensive.*

HOLMENKOLLEN RESTAURANT
Holmenkollvn. 119. Tel: 14-62-26.
Famed for its lunch time *koldtbord.* Lovely setting near the Holmenkollen ski jump. *Moderate.*

NAJADEN RESTAURANT
Bygdøynesvn 37. Tel: 43-81-80.
Part of the Maritime Museum on Bygdøy. See Oslo Itinerary 3. *Inexpensive* to *Moderate.*

RESTAURANT BLOM
Karl Johans Gate 41B. Tel: 42-73-00.
Over a hundred years old and carefully reconstructed. Try reindeer or seafood. *Expensive.*

STORTORVETS
Gjæstgiveri Grensen 1. Tel: 42-88-63.
Traditional old inn. Jazz on Friday and jazz café at lunch time. See Oslo Itinerary 3. *Inexpensive* to *Moderate.*

SYDVESTEN
Kirkegate 30. Tel: 33-34-42.
North Norwegian specialities, fish and game, cosy restaurant decorated with old fishing gear. Also **DYRY** bar. *Moderate.*

TAJ MAHAL
St Olavsgate 10. Tel: 36-21-15.
Tandoori Indian restaurant. Claims to offer the best value three-course meal in town. *Inexpensive.*

THEATERCAFÉEN (HOTEL CONTINENTAL)
Stortingsgate 24–26. Tel: 33-32-00.
Famous haunt of artists, actors and the intelligentsia. See Oslo Itinerary 3. *Moderate.*

VEGETA VERTSHUS
Munkedamsvn. 3.
Tel: 83-42-32/83-40-20.
Oslo's leading vegetarian restaurant. Excellent value. *Inexpensive.*

At your service

Bergen

AUGUSTIN
Sundtsgate 24. Tel: 23-00-25.
A popular bistro in the Augustin Hotel. Fish specialities. *Moderate.*

AUGUSTUS
*Galleriet shopping mall,
Torgalmenningen. Tel: 32-35-25.*
See Bergen Itinerary 2. *Inexpensive.*

BANCO ROTTO
Vågsalmenningen 16. Tel: 32-75-20.
Magnificent interior. Restaurant, piano bar, *konditori*, and pub. Prices range from inexpensive to expensive according to which restaurant you choose.

BELLEVUE
Bellevuebakken 9. Tel: 31-02-40.
An elegant restaurant with a superb view over the city. See Bergen Itinerary 2. *Expensive.*

BRYGGESTUEN and BRYGGELOFTET
Bryggen. Tel: 31-06-30.
Two restaurants in one of the old Hanseatic wharfhouses with a good atmosphere. A mecca for most visitors. *Moderate.*

BRYGGEN TRACTEURSTED
Bryggen. Tel: 31-40-46.
Right in the heart of the earliest Bryggen houses, with outside garden. Billed as 'the oldest tavern in Norway.' *Inexpensive* to *Moderate.*

FISKEKROGEN
Zachariasbryggen. Tel: 31-75-66.
See Bergen Itinerary 1. *Moderate.*

ENHJØRNINGEN
Bryggen. Tel: 32-79-19.
A wharfhouse fish and seafood restaurant. See Bergen Itinerary 1. *Moderate.*

GRILLEN HOTEL NORGE
Ole Bulls Plass. Tel: 21-01-00.
A first-class gourmet restaurant. Excellent food, good service. *Expensive.*

**OLE BULL RESTAURANT
(HOTEL NORGE)**
Tel: 21-01-00.
Superb *koldtbord* from noon–6pm, also light meals and à la carte. *Inexpensive to moderate.*

ØL OG VIN STUE
Ole Bulls Plass. Tel: 90-07-70.
Bergen's largest restaurant houses six bars, including Rock and Roll, disco, beer/winebar, casino, and Maxime's nightclub. *Inexpensive.*

SAS ROYAL HOTEL
Stadsraaden, Bryggen. Tel: 54-30-00.
Gourmet restaurant. *Expensive.*

MADAM FELLE (SAS ROYAL HOTEL)
Tel: 54-30-00.
An old Bergen-style tap room, wine, beer and light meals. *Inexpensive.*

TO KOKKER
Enhjørningssgården. Tel: 32-28-16.
Sister restaurant to Enhjørningen, offering meat as well as fish. Set in old wharfhouse, in a series of small rooms. *Moderate.*

Nightlife

In summer, the light lingers so long in Norway that it seems a crime to go inside. Perhaps this is the reason that night time entertainment arrived here late. A more likely explanation is the ferocity of former anti-drinking laws, the residue of a strict Lutheran piety that led to prohibition in World War I. Outlawing of alcohol continued into the 1920s and only a change of government brought about its repeal. From that time, the state has had a monopoly on all imports of wines and spirits, and also runs Vinmonopolet (alcohol shops) where you buy alcohol

at a high price in an atmosphere like that of a doctor's waiting room.

The Norwegians did not have much incentive to nightlife in the sense of pubs and late drinking until the 1980s, when the loosening of drink laws brought a remarkable change. Though there was no reduction in prices, oil-rich Norwegians, at least in the cities, plunged into a style of life that extended into the small hours. Before then, with dinner, concert or cinema over, there was little left to do in the evening other than return to the hotel for a nightcap. The concept of 'buying a round' hardly existed. Even today in some groups of friends each person will buy his or her own drink.

With the relaxation of drinking restrictions, hotels have gradually begun to add nightclubs, and the disco age, particularly in Oslo, has brought a sudden rush of discos/pubs/cafés which stay open until the early hours. Nowadays, they open and close and change their names and their owners with such speed that it is risky to recommend any but the most established.

At the same time, these late-night establishments are not night-clubs in the expected sense that people will be dressy and the sur-

Smile . . . it's Saturday night

roundings luxurious. They are more in the style of pubs where you can probably dance and always drink late.

If you like a pre-dinner drink, the best advice is to take in your full duty-free allowance and make your own in your room. Norwegian hotel mini-bars are, by law, only allowed to stock wines, beer and soft drinks. Your own bottle is not much help in a restaurant or club and there is no practical way of getting over the price of alcohol outside. Bars and discos always serve coffee or tea and are quite happy if you stick to these options while listening to the music or dancing. The drink-driving laws are fierce; the only safe answer is not to drink any alcohol when in charge of a car. A familiar sight on a Saturday and Sunday morning is a Norwegian walking back to pick up his vehicle from where he left it the night before.

In a Norwegian home it is a different matter. There is usually no visible shortage of spirits and the host will certainly offer a wide choice, particularly of *akvavit* (see *Eating Out*), that has never seen Vinmonopolet: home distilling is widespread. Recipes and flavourings are swopped and it is relatively easy to buy essences to give the different tastes. Though home distilling is strictly illegal and there are checks, plenty of it goes on.

Oslo and Bergen both have symphony orchestras and their concert halls play host to many artistes outside the classical world. Oslo has the National Theatre, though plays are mostly in Norwegian, and the cities and bigger towns have cinemas. Scandinavians rarely dub English-language programmes but use sub-titles, Sunday evening is the great cinema evening. Outside the cities, nightlife in the club sense is almost non-existent though hotels often provide evening entertainment in the summer and during the winter skiing seasons.

Oslo

Always check with the *Oslo Guide* and *What's On In Oslo* for nightclubs and discos, as they open and close with such rapidity. The following list gives a few well-established venues and most big hotels have some kind of club or late-night bar.

CHAGALL (VICTORIA)
Karl Johans Gate 35. Tel: 42-97-10.
Open until 2am Friday, 4am Saturday. Disco every night. Lower age limit is 20 years.

The Grieghallen

CRUISE KAFÉ
Aker Brygge 1. Tel: 41-03-69.
One of many in Aker Brygge. Good changing bands. Usually packed.

FRU BLOM BLOM'S
Karl Johans Gate 39–41. Tel: 42-73-00.
Bodega-style club with wine by the glass. Open until 12.30am, Friday/Saturday until 1.30am.

EILEFS LANDHANDLERI
Kristian IV's Gate opposite the Bristol Hotel. Tel: 42-53-47.
Fine pub with music and dancing un-

til 4am.
GALAXY NIGHT CLUB (SAS HOTEL)
Holbergsgate 30. Tel: 30-01-66.
Swinging Tuesday through to Saturday until 4am.

PRIVATEN NIGHTCLUB
Grensen 1. Tel: 42-88-63.
Beer and wine. Dancing until 4am.

ROCKEFELLER
Torgata 16. Tel: 20-32-32.
One of Oslo's best known clubs. Mar-

vellous setting in the old Torgata baths. International musicians during the many festivals. Occasional concerts. Lower age limit 20 years for normal admission, for concerts 18.

SHEKK INN
Grensen. Tel: 42-86-83.
Wednesday–Saturday until 2am, Friday jazz and dancing.

SMUGET
Kirkegate 34. Tel: 43-52-02.
Oslo's music joint 'through the alley' (*smuget*). Meals are à la carte until 3.15am and live jazz, blues and rock until 4am every night.

Bergen
If you're drinking alcohol, there is no way of nightclubbing inexpensively. Hotels Norge, (**PANDORA**), Rosenkrantz (**RUBINEN**) and SAS Royal (**ENGELEN**) all have nightclubs, which stay open until 3am.

BANCO ROTTO
Vågsalmenningen. Tel: 32-75-20.
Music, dancing in an elegant setting. 10pm–2.30am Friday and Saturday.

CHRISTIAN
Chr. Michelsensgate 4. Tel: 32-02-62.
Popular and well-patronised. Nightly until 2am, Friday and Saturday, until 2.30am.

HOLM'S
Kong Oscarsgate 45. Tel: 31-59-30.
Late-night eating, drinking, music and dancing. Thursday, Friday and Saturday, 9pm–3am.

MAXIME
Øl og Vin building. Tel: 90-07-70.
Licensed for wine and beer. Nightly until 3am.

Calendar of Special Events

The Norwegian passion for the open air and 'the nature' means that many of the best annual events are sporting: skiing and ski-jumping in winter, and fishing and other outdoor festivals in summer. Street races and cycle marathons are also popular. At the end of June, Oslo turns out to welcome the competitors in **Den Store Styrkeprøven** cycle marathon from Trondheim. In May, Bergen has its **7 Fjellsturen**, an enthusiastic mountain walk over the city's seven hills. In March there is Oslo's famous ski festival, the **Holmenkollen Festival,** which attracts thousands out to the great ski jump in the Nordmarka. In the summer, the city's Bislett Stadium is the venue for an international athletics meeting, the **Mobil Bislett Games**.

Norwegians celebrate their **Constitution Day** on 17 May with enormous zeal but, thankfully, no displays of military might: just children who appear as a kaleidoscope of red, white and blue under the waving flags.

The biggest celebrations are in Oslo, concentrated around Karl Johans Gate, leading up to the Royal Palace. But each community will have its own distinctive festivities and, in Bergen, a lively and important part of the parade is the Buekorps, an association similar to the Boys' Brigade.

Midtsommer on 23 June is often a family party though there are also public celebrations. Their dark northern winters lead Scandinavians almost to worship the light. The centrepiece today is still the bonfire, around which people eat, drink, dance, sing, play games and stay up late on what is the lightest night of the year.

Bergen can claim the biggest arts festival in Norway, the **Bergen International Festival** in May and June. The festival, which started in the early 1950s, emphasises classical and other music but there is also theatre and bal-

Carnival in Bergen

let. The focal point is the Grieghallen, named after Norway's most famous composer, but there are many other venues. A **Night Jazz Festival**, a **Children's Festival**, and traditional folk music and dancing take place at the same time. Oslo also has a **Jazz Festival** in August.

Norwegian national holidays are: Easter; Labour Day (1 May); Constitution Day (17 May); Ascension Day; Whitsun; Christmas and Boxing Day and New Year's Day. The lists below give the main events in each city.

OSLO

January–February
Lillehammer Ski Festival (January). Entertainment and contests in Lillehammer, 1½ hours north of Oslo.

March
Holmenkollen Ski Festival.

May–June
Summer Kollen (June). Concerts, classical, pop, jazz and other entertainment around Holmenkollen Ski Jump.
Midtsommer (23 June). Midsummer.
Den Store Styrkeprøven (end June). Cycle marathon, Trondheim to Oslo.

July–August
Mobil Bislett Games (July), international athletics at Bislett Stadium.
Jazz Festival and concerts.
The Norway Cup, international youth soccer with 1,000 teams of boys and girls, held in Ekeberg.
Maridalspelet (mid-August). Open-

air historical drama, takes place in church ruins at Maridalen.

September–October
National Autumn Exhibition (September). New graphic art, painting, sculpture, Kunstnershus.
Oslo Marathon (September).
Contemporary Music Festival (Oct).

November–December
Nobel Peace Prize awarded in the University Aula (December).
Winter Olympics (1994), to be held in Lillehammer, north of Oslo.

BERGEN

May–June
Bergen International Festival and **Night Jazz Festival** and **Exhibition**.
Midtsommer (23 June). Midsummer.

May–August
Art Exhibition. Exhibition and demonstration of old Norwegian culture and crafts, held in Rosendal.

July–September
Fishing Festival (early July) in the city centre.
North Sea Festival (mid-July). Historical festival.
Grieg Concerts at Troldhaugen, the composer's home.
Concerts also take place at Ole Bull's home at Lysøen.
Rosendal Barony Concerts at Bergen (July).
Baronispelet, drama at Rosendal.
Norwegian Film Festival (August).

Practical Information

GETTING THERE

By Air

Scandinavian Air Systems (SAS), operated jointly by Denmark, Norway and Sweden, flies into Fornebu Airport, Oslo, from most major European cities, as do many other national airlines. Norway Airlines (part of TransNordic Group) also flies to Oslo

from London. Bergen's Flesland Airport is also easily reached, either directly or via Oslo. Both airports have bus services into the centre.

Within Norway, the air network is remarkable. The main carrier is Braathens but even tiny airports are served by Norving, NorskAir or Widerøe.

By Rail

International trains arrive at Oslo Sentral (Oslo-S) from all over Europe, and Norwegian State Railways (NSB) provides a comprehensive and efficient internal network. Even the worst winter weather rarely stops the Oslo/Bergen line.

The NSB head office is at Jernbanetorget 1 (Tel: 36-37-80). In Bergen, the station is on Strømgaten, (Tel: 31-94-40 or 31-93-05).

By Sea

Oslo car ferries run to and from Copenhagen, Kiel, Hirtshals (Denmark) and Fredrikshavn (Denmark).

Bergen car ferries arrive from and depart to Newcastle (Britain), the Faroe Islands and Iceland.

By Road

Formalities on most border crossings are swift and, once you are in Scandinavia, almost non-existent. Both Bergen and Oslo make a modest charge for bringing a car into the city centre, which is collected at toll booths.

Do *not* drink and drive. Penalties are savage (up to 10,000NKR, and in some cases even imprisonment) and the limit very low (0.5ml). A half-litre (just under a pint) of beer could

be too much. Norwegian medicines to be avoided before driving are marked with a red triangle.

TRAVEL ESSENTIALS

Passports and Visas
For the citizens of most countries, a valid passport is all that is required. From the rest of Scandinavia, plus Iceland and Finland, emigration officers do not even stamp passports.

Customs, Excise and Duty Free
Visitors over the age of 20 can bring in one litre of spirits and one litre of wine, or two litres of wine, plus two litres of beer. Europeans over 16 years of age can bring in 200 cigarettes or 250g tobacco. Visitors over 16 from non-European countries may bring 400 cigarettes or 500g tobacco. One kilo of chocolate and sweets is allowed, and other goods up to 1,000 NKR, though items for personal use are usually excluded.

Time Zone
Scandinavian time is Central European, one hour ahead of Greenwich Mean Time, and six ahead of Eastern Standard Time. Summer time (when the clock is put forward one hour) lasts from the end of March through to September.

Telephone and Post
Many hotels have direct dial telephones (surcharged) and many have fax facilities. You can also make overseas calls from phone boxes or from main telegraph offices.

Central Post Offices, Oslo: Dronningensgt 15, Oslo 1. Bergen: Main Post Office, Byparken. To call other countries, first dial the international access code 095, then the relevant country code: Australia (61); France (33); Germany (49); Italy (39); Japan (81); Netherlands (31); Spain (34); United Kingdom (44); US and Canada (1). If you are using a US credit phone card, dial the company's access number below, followed by the country code etc. Sprint: Tel: 050-12877; AT&T, Tel: 050-12011; MCI, Tel: 050-12912.

Directory Enquiries and Codes
For numbers in Norway and Scandinavia, dial 0180; other countries 0181; telegrams, 0138. Phone books have an instruction page in English.

Norway's international code is 47. City code for Oslo is 02 and Bergen is 05 (the 0 is dropped when phoning from outside Norway). City codes are not used within their own areas.

Climate
In Oslo, winter day temperatures average -2°C (28°F) and 5° less at night. Bergen is slightly warmer but wetter and snow rarely lies heavily for long. Average summer temperatures for the whole country are around 16°C (60°F) and in Oslo around 22°C (71°F).

What to Wear

Norwegians dress informally and women wear trousers for everything but the most formal occasions. For men, it is wise, but not obligatory, to carry a tie. In summer, light clothes with a cover-up, plus sturdy shoes/boots an anorak or raincoat and an umbrella are wise precautions.

The winter calls for very warm clothes. Norwegian hotels and houses are comfortingly warm so use the layers method of dressing, and add and subtract as necessary. Mitts, gloves, warm caps are essential, as also are sunglasses or goggles for summer sun and winter snow, particularly for sailing and skiing.

MONEY MATTERS

The currency is the Norwegian krone (NKR) divided into 100 øre. Notes are in 50, 100, 500 and 1,000 denominations; coins in 1, 5, 10.

You can bring unlimited amounts of currency into Norway but cannot take out more than 5,000NKR (plus the money you brought in).

Banks, post offices, airports, bigger hotels, foreign exchange bureaux in Oslo and Tourist Information Centres in Oslo and Bergen, change foreign currency, traveller's cheques and Eurocheques; most banks will issue cash against credit cards. Carry reasonably high value traveller's cheques because you pay a charge on each cheque, not on each transaction.

Banking hours are 8.15am–3.30pm, Thursday to 5pm. Closed weekends.

GETTING AROUND

Public Transport

Oslo has an excellent and well-integrated public transport service. The *Oslo Guide* is sensible and easy to follow, with careful explanations.

There are eight underground lines (SST) which converge at Stortinget, and five tram routes. Bus routes all converge on Jernbanetorget. Ferries connect the Oslofjord islands to the mainland from Vippertangen (bus 29 from Jernbanetorget) and the Bygdøy ferry leaves from Pier 3 outside the Rådhuset. For transport queries, telephone Trafikanten at Jernbanetorget (Tel: 17-70-30, Monday–Friday 7am–8pm, Saturday–Sunday 8am–6pm).

Oslo Taxicentral can be telephoned on 38-80-90, and advance bookings (over one hour) made on 38-80-80.

Bergen has a good network of well-integrated bus services within the city and to the surrounding area. Ferries are also included. Consult *HSD Rutehefte*, free from the HSD Transport Company, Strandgaten 191 (Tel: 23-87-00) or at local ferries and bus stations. The Central Bus Station at Strømgaten (Tel: 32-67-80) is the terminal for all services to the Bergen environs and the airport bus. There is no special visitor bus ticket but you can buy a 48-hour unlimited bus travel ticket, available on the buses.

Bergen has no internal train service (only the summertime road-train, Bergen Express, designed for visitors). Main-line trains from Oslo and stations en route arrive and depart at the Strømgaten Station (Tel: 31-96-40/31-93-05). There are funicular railways to two of Bergen's seven hills, Fløien and Ulriken.

Ferries cross Vågen from Bryggen (below Rosenkrantztårnet) to the Nordnes peninsula, 7am–4.15pm on weekdays only and from Nøstekaien, on the Puddefjorden side of Nordnes. Other local boats serving the islands north of Bergen dock at Strandkaiterminalen, the inner harbour on the left-hand side of the fish market. The *Hurtigrute* (coastal steamer) and boats for fjords to the north leave from the Puddefjord inner harbour to the south-west of the centre. All quays are clearly marked in the *Bergen Guide* and on the local map.

Private Car
It is crazy to use a car in central Oslo, but for journeys outside it can be helpful. Good motoring maps for the Greater Oslo area available from the Tourist Information Centre.
Oslo Car Hire: Avis, Billingstadsletta 14 (Tel: 84-90-60). Also look under *Bilutleie* in the telephone directory, or ask at hotels and the Tourist Information Centre.
Breakdown Service: Falken (Tel: 23-25-85); NAF Alarmsentral (Tel: 34-16-00) or Viking (Tel: 31-01-00). All operate a 24-hour service.

There is no particular advantage in having a car in the centre of Bergen, though the one-way system is well-

marked and effective. There is a toll charge, which is paid on entry. Outside the city, a car is more flexible than the bus, but is not a necessity.
Bergen Car Hire: Hertz, Nygårdsgaten 89 (Tel: 32-79-20). Also look under *Bilutleie* in the telephone directory, or ask at hotels and the Tourist Information Centre.
Breakdown Service: Viking Salvage Corps, Edvard Griegsvei 3 (Tel: 29-22-22). 24-hour service.

Oslokartet
The **Oslo Card** gives free travel on virtually all public transport in the city, and suburban and NSB (main railway) trains within the Greater Oslo area. It also provides free parking in municipal car parks plus discounts on museum entrance prices.

ACCOMMODATION

Norwegian hotels are almost without exception of good standard. Geared to business use in the cities, they are expensive but provide swimming pools and fitness and other facilities. Almost all cut their prices dramatically from mid-June, through July and most of August. Weekend rates are also frequently slashed.

If you have been unable to book in advance, the Tourist Information Centres in Oslo at Vestbanestasjonen (Tel: 33-43-86), Oslo S (Tel: 17-11-24), and Bergen (Tel: 32-14-80) will book accommodation, charging a small fee. In Oslo, Oslo Hotel Booking, Grensen 5–7 (Tel: 42-62-62), will book hotels throughout Scandinavia with no booking fee.

Oslo
Hotel prices at the top end are marginally higher than Bergen's and present difficulties of categorisation because of seasonal variations, weekend

rates etc. Be sure to ask for the full range and not just the standard price before you book. A rough guide for two sharing per night: *Expensive*: 1,000NKR-plus; *Moderate*: 600–1,000 NKR; *Inexpensive*: less than 600NKR.

BRISTOL
Kristian IV's Gate 7. Tel: 41-58-40.
A famous hotel, with ornate lobby. Antiques feature in bedrooms and public rooms. Renowned *koldtbord*. *Expensive*.

CONTINENTAL
Stortingsgate 24–26. Tel: 41-90-60.
A beautiful hotel opposite the National Theatre, with two famous restaurants. *Expensive*.

GRAND
Karl Johans Gate 31. Tel: 42-93-90.
Ibsen's favourite haunt. Luxury hotel with rooftop swimming pool, and Grand Café overlooking the Storting. *Expensive*.

HOLMENKOLLEN PARK HOTEL
Rica Kongevn 26. Tel: 14-60-90.
A traditional Norwegian building near Holmenkollen Ski Jump, and only some 15 minutes by underground train to Stortinget. *Moderate*.

NORUM HOTEL
Bygdøy Allé. Tel: 44-79-90.
On the west side of the city within walking distance of Frogner (Vige-land) Park; 10 minutes by bus to the centre. Excellent small restaurant, popular also with non-residents. *Inexpensive*.

ROYAL CHRISTIANIA
Biskop Gunnerusgate 3. Tel: 42-94-10.
Beautifully modernised from an earlier hotel, with huge central atrium, excellent service, fine breakfast board. Close to Oslo Sentral station. *Expensive* but ask about weekend rates.

Bergen

Bergen hotels are only marginally less expensive than Oslo's but prices vary enormously throughout the year. The following categories may help. They cover two people sharing a double room, usually with a lavish breakfast. *Expensive*: 1,000NKR and over. *Moderate:* 500–1,000NKR. *Inexpensive*: below 500NKR.

ADMIRAL HOTEL
Sundtsgate 9–13. Tel: 32-47-30.
Down by the water looking over the harbour to Bryggen, with a good restaurant, called Emily. *Expensive*.

AUGUSTIN HOTEL
Sundtsgate 24. Tel: 23-00-25.
On Vågen, close to the ferry over to Bergenhus. Known for good food. Beer and wine licence only. *Moderate*.

BERGEN GJESTEHUS
Vestre Torvgate 20. Tel: 31-96-66.
On the hill towards Johanneskirke, good position looking down to Torgalmenningen. Licensed for wine and beer. *Inexpensive*.

KLOSTER PENSION
Klosteret 12. Tel: 90-21-58.
In classic old district on Nordnes peninsula, well-modernised. Good breakfast included. *Inexpensive*.

Hotel Norge
Ole Bulls Plass 4. Tel: 21-01-00.
One of Bergen's most famous and well-loved hotels. Four restaurants including the gourmet Grillen. Night club, indoor pool, winter garden. *Expensive.*

Hotel Rosenkrantz
Rosenkrantzgaten 7. Tel: 31-50-00.
Comfortable hotel in classic early 20th-century building, well-modernised. Close to Bryggen. Restaurant, piano bar and nightclub. *Moderate.*

SAS Royal Hotel
Bryggen. Tel: 54-30-00.
Built into several old wharfhouses, with entrance close to Bryggensmuseum. High standard of facilities. Airport bus to Flesland outside. *Expensive.*

Victoria Kong
Oscarsgate 29. Tel: 31-50-30.
An old staging-post inn with 43 well-modernised and comfortable rooms. Very central, good value. *Moderate.*

HEALTH & EMERGENCIES

No vaccinations are needed. Norway has reciprocal arrangements for health treatment with most European countries. From Great Britain obtain form E111 from a Post Office before you go. Charges are relatively small.

Emergency Medical Treatment

Oslo
OSLO KOMMUNALE LEGEVAKT
Storgaten 40, Tel: 20-10-90 (24hrs).

Emergency Dental Treatment

Oslo
OSLO KOMMUNALE TANNLEGEVAKT
Tøyen Senter, Kolstadgata 18.
Tel: 67-48-46.
Weekdays 8am–11pm. Saturday, Sunday and holidays 11am–2pm, 8–11pm.

Bergen
30 Lars Hillesgate
Tel: 32-11-20.
Daily 10–11am, 7–9pm.

Duty Chemist

Oslo
JERNBANETORGETS APOTEK
Jernbanetorget 4B, Oslo 1
Tel: 41-24-82 (24hrs).

Bergen
APOTEKET NORDSTJERNEN
Bus Station
Tel: 31-68-84 (24hrs).

Emergency Numbers
Police 002
Fire 001
Accident/Ambulance 003

ACTIVITIES

Skating
Oslo Kommune has some 150 winter skating rinks, and you can hire speed, ice and figure skates. Natural ice rinks are usually open from the beginning of December through March.

Curling
There are several curling clubs in Oslo which welcome members of foreign clubs: Oslo Curlingskrets (Tel: 22-95-05) or Norwegian Curling Association (Tel: 51-88-00).

Sledging
A horse-drawn sledge ride in the Oslo forest is one of the highlights of any winter visit. Contact: Vangen Skistue, c/o Laila and John Hamre, Fjell, 1404 Siggerud (Tel: 09-86-54-81) or Sørbråten Gård, c/o Helge Torp, 0890 Maridalen (Tel: 02-42-35-79). An alternative is to try your hand at a dog-sledge. For lunchtime and evening tours contact: Norske Sledehundturer, Einar Kristen Aas, 1500 Moss (Tel: 09-27-37-86 or 094-53-341).

Trotting
A popular sport in both cities. Oslo's track is at Bjerke Travbane (Tel: 64-60-50). Bergen's is at Haukås in Åsane (Tel: 24-79-00).

Swimming
Though you should not swim right inside Oslo's inner harbour, summer swimming in the fjord and off the islands is very popular. There are also many public swimming pools.

Bergen Sports Clubs

Fishing
BERGEN SPORTSFISKERE
Fosswinekelsgate. Tel: 32-11-64.

Tennis
BERGEN TENNIS CLUB
Årstad. Tel: 29-91-67.

Sailing
BERGEN YACHTING CLUB
Hjellestad. Tel: 22-65-45.

USEFUL ADDRESSES

Norwegian Tourist Boards

Great Britain
NORWEGIAN TOURIST BOARD
*5–11 Lower Regent Street,
London SW1Y 4LR.*

United States of America
NORWEGIAN TOURIST BOARD
*655 Third Avenue,
New York, NY 10017.*

Sweden
NORSKA TURISTBYRÅN
*World Trade Centre, Str S4 1251,
Gothenburg.*

Denmark
NORGES TURISTKONTO
*Trondhjems Plads 4, DK-2100
Copenhagen.*

Finland
NORGES TURISTBYRÅ
*Georgsgatan (Yrjönkatu) 23,
P709, SF-00101 Helsinki.*

Germany/Switzerland/Austria
NORWEGISCHES FREMDENVERKEHRSAMT
*Norwegen Zentrum,
Mundsburger Damm 27, D-2000
Hamburg 76.*

France
OFFICE NATIONALE DU TOURISME DE
NORVEGE
*88 Ave. Charles de Gaulle,
F-92200 Neuilly-sur-Seine.*

Netherlands, Belgium, Luxembourg
NOORS NATIONAAL VERKEERSBUREAU
*Saxen Weimarlaan 58,
NL-1075 CE Amsterdam.*

Sightseeing and Tours

HMK SIGHTSEEING
Tel: 20-82-06/20-83-02.
Oslo sightseeing by coach.

BÆTSERVICE SIGHTSEEING
Tel: 20-07-15.
Fjord sightseeing by boat and coach
from Oslo.

BHV/FYKSESUND FJORDRUTER
Tel: 55-53-33.
Day tours from Bergen to Hardanger
by bus and boat.

BNR – BERGEN-NORDHORDLAND
RUTELAG
Tel: 31-81-10.
Tours north from Bergen to fjords
and mountains of Nordhordland.

DE GULE BUSSENE
Tel: 28-13-30.   ·
Bergen bus tours.

FYLKESBAATENE I SOGN OG FJORDANE
Tel: 32-40-15.
Boat/train/bus tours north from
Bergen to the Sognefjord, including
'Norway in a Nutshell'.

HARDANGERTOUR
Tel: 55-53-33.
Minicruise in Hardanger, by bus and
boat from Bergen.

**HSD HARDANGER SUNNHORDLANDSKE
DAMPSKIPSSELSKAP**
Tel: 23-87-80/90.
Bus/ferry tours from Bergen to Har-
danger, Sunnhordland, Rosendal, etc.

TRAVEL SERVICE
Tel: 17-06-36.
Oslo sightseeing by coach.

UNITUR
Tel: 23-88-88.
Oslo bus tours.

WHITE LADY
Tel: 31-43-20/31-59-00.
Bergen fjord sightseeing.

Tourist and Other Services

BERGEN KOMMUNE (local authority)
Bergen City Hall. Tel: 97-60-56.
Information office, 11th floor.

TOURIST INFORMATION CENTRE
Vestbanestasjonen, Oslo.
Tel: 83-00-50.

TOURIST INFORMATION CENTRE
Oslo Sentral. Tel: 17-11-24.

GUIDE SERVICE
Oslo. Tel: 41-48-63.
Slottsgaten 1, Bergen. Tel: 32-77-00.
Also ask at travel agencies, and Tour-
ist Information Centres.

**OSLO REISELIVSRÅD
(OSLO PROMOTION)**
Grev Wedels Plass 2, Oslo.
Tel: 42-71-00.

NORWEGIAN TOURIST BOARD
Langdaia 1, Oslo. Tel: 42-70-44.

Embassies and Consulates

Oslo

Canada
Oscarsgate 20. Tel: 46-69-55.

Denmark
Olav Kyrresgate 7. Tel: 44-18-46.

France
Drammensvn. 69. Tel: 44-18-20.

Germany
Oscarsgate 45. Tel: 55-20-10.

Great Britain
Ths. Heftyesgate 8. Tel: 55-24-00.

Spain
Oscarsgate 35. Tel: 55-20-15.

Sweden
Noblesgate 16. Tel: 44-38-15.

United States of America
Drammensv. 18. Tel: 44-85-50.

Bergen

Denmark
Kalfarveien 57A. Tel: 31-10-30.

Finland
Jan Løken, c/o Den Norske Bank,
Torgalm 2. Tel: 21-13-71/21-12-09.

France
Sandbrugt 5. Tel: 31-04-61.

Germany
Johan K Troye, C Sundtsgate 60c.
Tel: 90-23-65.

Sweden
Olav Kyrresgate. Tel: 31-60-32.

Index

Art & Photo Credits

14, 21, 22, 23, 24T, 28B, 39, 40, 42T, **Hauke Dressler**
52B, 68B, 79

24B, 27, 30, 35, 42B, 43T, 61B, 65B, **Fritz Dressler**
68T, 72T, 83T

Cover, 46, 47, 48B, 53, 59B, 66, 67, 69B, **Tor Eigeland**
72B, 80, 84, 88T, 89

8–9, 10, 15T, 25, 31, 32, 33, 38, 48T, **Nor-Ice Library**
49, 54, 55B, 61T, 62–3, 76

20, 51B, 56B, 63, 70, 83B **Tony McCann**

4–5, 11, 16, 26, 34B, 37, 51T, 71, 73, **Topham Picture Source**

56T, 64, 65T, 90 **Anthony R Dalton**

69T, 88B **Aslak Aarhus**

12 **Trygve Bølstad**

15 **Robert Meyer Collection**

77B **Stefan Hanberg**

55T **Terje Bergesen**

74T **Nigel Tisdall**

Managing Editor **Andrew Eames**
Design Concept **V Barl**
Design **Gareth Walters**
Cover Design **Klaus Geisler**
Cartography **Berndtson & Berndtson**